Teach Yourself VISUALLY™

Digital Photography
2nd Edition

by Charlotte K. Lowrie

Visual

From

maranGraphics®

&

Wiley Publishing, Inc.

Teach Yourself VISUALLY™ Digital Photography 2nd Edition

Published by
Wiley Publishing, Inc.
111 River Street
Hoboken, NJ 07030-5774

Published simultaneously in Canada

Library of Congress Control Number:

ISBN: 0-7645-5596-0

Manufactured in the United States of America

10 9 8 7 6 5 4 3 2 1

2K/SS/RS/QT/IN

Trademark Acknowledgments

Important Numbers

For U.S. corporate orders, please call maranGraphics at 800-469-6616 or fax 905-890-9434.

For general information on our other products and services or to obtain technical support please contact our Customer Care Department within the U.S. at 800-762-2974, outside the U.S. at 317-572-3993 or fax 317-572-4002.

Permissions

Wiley Publishing, Inc.

U.S. Corporate Sales	**U.S. Trade Sales**
Contact maranGraphics at (800) 469-6616 or Fax (905) 890-9434.	Contact Wiley at (800) 762-2974 or Fax (317) 572-4002.

Some comments from our readers...

"I have to praise you and your company on the fine products you turn out. I have twelve of the *Teach Yourself VISUALLY* and *Simplified* books in my house. They were instrumental in helping me pass a difficult computer course. Thank you for creating books that are easy to follow."

— *Gordon Justin (Brielle, NJ)*

"I commend your efforts and your success. I teach in an outreach program for the Dr. Eugene Clark Library in Lockhart, TX. Your *Teach Yourself VISUALLY* books are incredible, and I use them in my computer classes. All my students love them!"

— *Michele Schalin (Lockhart, TX)*

"Like a lot of other people, I understand things best when I see them visually. Your books really make learning easy and life more fun."

— *John T. Frey (Cadillac, MI)*

"I have quite a few of your Visual books and have been very pleased with all of them. I love the way the lessons are presented!"

— *Mary Jane Newman (Yorba Linda, CA)*

"I write to extend my thanks and appreciation for your books. They are clear, easy to follow, and straight to the point. Keep up the good work!"

— *Seward Kollie (Dakar, Senegal)*

"I am an avid fan of your Visual books. If I need to learn anything, I just buy one of your books and learn the topic in no time. Wonders! I have even trained my friends to give me Visual books as gifts."

— *Illona Bergstrom (Aventura, FL)*

"Thank you for making it so clear. I appreciate it. I will buy many more Visual books."

— *J.P. Sangdong (North York, Ontario, Canada)*

"I was introduced to maranGraphics about four years ago and YOU ARE THE GREATEST THING THAT EVER HAPPENED TO INTRODUCTORY COMPUTER BOOKS!"

— *Glenn Nettleton (Huntsville, AL)*

"Compliments to the chef!! Your books are extraordinary! Or, simply put, extra-ordinary, meaning way above the rest! THANK YOU THANK YOU THANK YOU! for creating these."

— *Christine J. Manfrin (Castle Rock, CO)*

"I just purchased my third Visual book (my first two are dog-eared now!) and, once again, your product has surpassed my expectations. The expertise, thought, and effort that go into each book are obvious, and I sincerely appreciate your efforts. Keep up the wonderful work!"

— *Tracey Moore (Memphis, TN)*

"Thank you, thank you, thank you...for making it so easy for me to break into this high-tech world. I now own four of your books. I recommend them to anyone who is a beginner like myself. Now...if you could just do one for programming VCR's, it would make my day!"

— *Gay O'Donnell (Calgary, Alberta, Canada)*

"You're marvelous! I am greatly in your debt."

— *Patrick Baird (Lacey, WA)*

maranGraphics is a family-run business located near Toronto, Canada.

At **maranGraphics**, we believe in producing great computer books — one book at a time.

maranGraphics has been producing high-technology products for over 25 years, which enables us to offer the computer book community a unique communication process.

Our computer books use an integrated communication process, which is very different from the approach used in other computer books. Each spread is, in essence, a flow chart — the text and screen shots are totally incorporated into the layout of the spread.

Introductory text and helpful tips complete the learning experience.

maranGraphics' approach encourages the left and right sides of the brain to work together — resulting in faster orientation and greater memory retention.

Above all, we are very proud of the handcrafted nature of our books. Our carefully-chosen writers are experts in their fields, and spend countless hours researching and organizing the content for each topic. Our artists rebuild every screen shot to provide the best

clarity possible, making our screen shots the most precise and easiest to read in the industry. We strive for perfection, and believe that the time spent handcrafting each element results in the best computer books money can buy.

Thank you for purchasing this book. We hope you enjoy it!

Sincerely,

Robert Maran
President
maranGraphics
Rob@maran.com
www.maran.com

CREDITS

Project Editor
Timothy J. Borek

Acquisitions Editor
Jody Lefevere

Product Development Manager
Lindsay Sandman

Copy Editor
Marylouise Wiack

Technical Editor
Joseph Wahman

Editorial Manager
Robyn Siesky

Permissions Editor
Carmen Krikorian

Manufacturing
Allan Conley
Linda Cook
Paul Gilchrist
Jennifer Guynn

Screen Artist
Jill A. Proll

Illustrators
Ronda David Burroughs
David E. Gregory
Sean Johanneson
Clint Lahnen
Russ Marini
Steven Shaerer

Book Design
maranGraphics®

Production Coordinator
Nancee Reeves

Layout and Graphics
Sean Decker
Carrie Foster
LeAndra Hosier
Kristin McMullan
Lynsey Osborn

Proofreaders
Jennifer Connolly

Quality Control
John Tyler Connoley
John Greenough
Susan Moritz

Indexer
Tom Dinse

Special Help
Judy Lefevere
Lindsay Sandman
Maureen Spears
Jade Williams

Vice President and Executive Group Publisher
Richard Swadley

Vice President and Publisher
Barry Pruett

Composition Director
Debbie Stailey

ABOUT THE AUTHOR

Charlotte K. Lowrie is a Seattle-based writer and photographer, is the managing editor of MSN Photos content (http://photos.msn.com/home.aspx). Her writing and photography have been published in magazines, including *Walking* and *Texas Highways;* newspapers, including the *Dallas Morning News,* and in technical books, help systems, and promotions for a variety of Microsoft products. You can visit her Web site at http://wordsandphotos.org.

AUTHOR'S ACKNOWLEDGMENTS

My sincere thanks to Tim Borek, project editor. This book is a testament to Tim's wise guidance and seemingly inexhaustable patience. Thanks also to Jody Lefevere, acquisitions editor, for your support. And thanks to Lindsay Sandman and her team of artists; Joe Wahman, technical editor; and Marylouise Wiack, copyeditor, for your insights and expertise. My thanks to the companies that allowed me to use, photograph, and mention their products and who answered technical questions along the way including Nikon, Fujifilm, Kodak, Olympus, Minolta, Microsoft, MSN Photos, and Lexar.

To my mother and my mentor, Margie Kissler.
Thank you for believing in me.

TABLE OF CONTENTS

Chapter 1

UNDERSTANDING DIGITAL PHOTOGRAPHY

Chapter 2

WHAT YOU NEED TO GET STARTED

Chapter 3

UNDERSTANDING LIGHT

Chapter 4

CONTROL EXPOSURE AND FOCAL LENGTH

Chapter 5

LEARN ABOUT FOCUS

Chapter 6

COMPOSE PICTURES LIKE A PRO

Chapter 7

PUT IT ALL TOGETHER

Chapter 8

TAKE YOUR FIRST DIGITAL PICTURES

TABLE OF CONTENTS

Chapter 9

AVOID DIGITAL PHOTOGRAPHY PITFALLS

Chapter 10

RETOUCH IMAGES IN PHOTOSHOP ELEMENTS

Chapter 11

CREATE EFFECTS

TABLE OF CONTENTS

Chapter 12

CROP, SIZE, AND SHARPEN PHOTOS

Chapter 13

PRINT PHOTOS

Chapter 14

SHARE PHOTOS ELECTRONICALLY

Chapter 15

CREATE PRINT PROJECTS

CHAPTER 1

Understanding Digital Photography

Are you confused about how digital photography works? This chapter introduces you to the advantages of digital photography, the different types of digital cameras, and how you can work with digital pictures.

★ *My Slideshow* ★ ★ ★ ★

WHY GO DIGITAL?

With digital photography, you can do more than take snapshots for your family album. You can use a digital camera to quickly and significantly improve your photography skills. You can e-mail your digital pictures to family and friends and simplify everyday tasks, such as illustrating a neighborhood newsletter.

Improve Your Photography Skills

Because digital pictures do not require film and processing, you can experiment with lighting, composition, camera modes, and creative techniques at no cost. Because you see images immediately, if an experiment yields poor results, you can delete the picture, modify your setting or approach, and try again. The best way to become a better photographer is to take many pictures.

Simplify Everyday Tasks

A digital camera allows you to share and convey information easily. For example, to illustrate steps for a friend on how to make a hobby project, you can photograph each step of the process and then send the pictures to your friend in an e-mail message or post them on a Web site. You can also take digital pictures of professional projects for use in your resume. Other tasks include creating a home inventory for insurance records and photographing items you are selling in online auctions.

Share Pictures Online and in E-mail

Within minutes of taking a picture, you can share it in an e-mail message, or upload it to a photo Web site to share with family and friends. Just choose the small size option on your camera to create pictures that are the ready to send in e-mail messages or to post on a Web site.

Create Photo Slideshows on CDs or DVDs

You can use programs, such as Ulead DVD PictureShow, to create digital image slideshows on recordable CDs and DVDs. Then add voice narration, captions, music, digital movie clips, and transitions to finish the slideshow. Some editing programs let you organize digital images by keywords and "ratings." You can use the keywords or ratings to select photos for your slideshow.

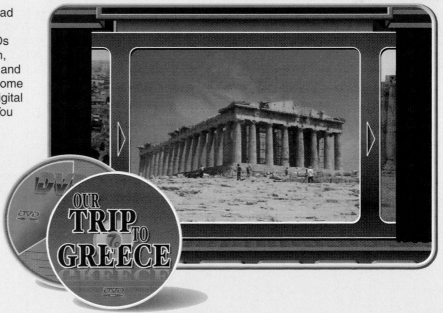

DISCOVER DIGITAL CAMERAS

When you understand how digital cameras work, you can make informed decisions when you purchase a camera. You can also get better images from the digital equipment that you are using.

How Digital Cameras Record Pictures

Digital cameras record pictures using an *image sensor array* — a grid composed of millions of light-sensitive *pixels*. A red, green, or blue filter covers each pixel so that it responds to only one of the primary colors of light. Each pixel absorbs the brightness and color in a scene to produce an electrical signal. The signal is then converted to a number that the camera's on-board computer analyzes to build a final image before storing it in memory.

Photo courtesy Olympus USA

Sensor   **Filter**

Types of Image Sensors

Most digital cameras use one of two types of image sensors: a Charge-Coupled Device (CCD), or a Complementary Metal-Oxide Semiconductor (CMOS). CCD sensors produce high-quality images with minimal *digital noise*, unwanted colored flecks in the picture.

While early CMOS images showed excessive digital noise, newer CMOS sensors eliminate most digital noise. More and more newer cameras feature CMOS sensors partly because CMOS sensor design offers opportunity for ongoing technological advances.

Resolution and Image Quality

Resolution is a measure of image quality; the higher the resolution, the finer the detail in the image. On a digital camera, the greater the number of pixels on the image sensor, the higher the resolution. Resolution is important for making photo-quality prints at 240 and 300 dots per inch, dpi, standard printing resolutions. The table below shows the minimum pixel width and height that a digital image should be to print at 300 dpi.

How Large Can I Print?

Print size (inches)	Minimum width (pixels)	Minimum height (pixels)
4 x 6	1200	1800
5 x 7	1050	750
8 x 10	1536	1024
11 x 14	1750	1375

*Note: You can print an acceptable 4"x 6" print from digital images that measure less than 1200 x 1800 pixels. However, the print resolution will be less than 300 dpi.

DISCOVER DIGITAL CAMERAS

File Formats and Compression

You can capture images in one of two or three file formats. JPEG, a *lossy* format, compresses or discards some image data to save space on memory cards. The higher the JPEG compression ratio, the more data is discarded. TIFF, a *lossless* format, retains all image data, and consequently, images consume more space. RAW format, or unprocessed image data, retains all image data but requires you to use a RAW conversion program.

It is best to select a lossless format or choose the highest JPEG setting with the lowest compression ratio.

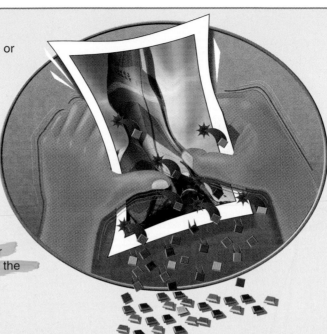

GIF

GIF files are most appropriate for use on Web pages of in e-mail. Although they use a lossless compression scheme and retain image information, they store only 256 colors. Prints can look rough or blotchy simply because they do not display enough shades of color to accurately reproduce an image. Using GIF89a, a variation of GIF, you can make portions of your image transparent and see a Web page background through the image.

BMP

Originally developed for use in Windows, this file type is used primarily for desktop wallpapers. The BMP file type does not resize well, so try not to use it with photographs.

More about Compression

While JPEG file compression allows you to fit more images on a memory card, to do so, it discards some image information during compression. To get the highest-quality prints, try to retain all or as much of the image information that the camera captures as possible. To do this using JPEG format, choose a high resolution and low-compression JPEG setting.

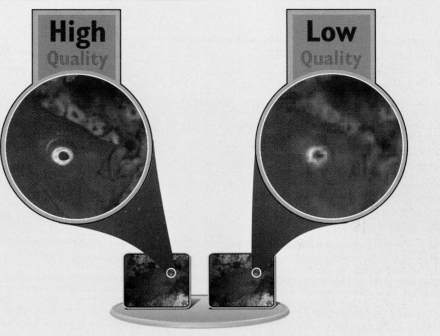

PICT

Only Macintosh computers can read PICT files. If you intend to share files between a PC and a Mac, use TIFF or JPEG.

PCD

PCD stands for PhotoCD, a format designed by Eastman Kodak for transferring slides and film negatives onto CD-ROM. Consumer image-editing software may be able to open these files, but they will not be able to save images in PCD format.

A digital workflow is a step-by-step process to help you get the best digital images and to manage your collection of images. The workflow includes taking, editing, sharing, organizing, and storing digital pictures. You can use the digital workflow described here as an introduction to and ongoing guide for working with your digital images.

Capture Images

The digital workflow begins by choosing camera settings and taking the picture. Choose a scene mode, a semi-automatic, automatic, or manual shooting mode.

Change the white balance to match the light in the scene. For more information on white balance, see Chapter 8.

Then you adjust zoom, focus, and take the picture. To learn more about exposure, see Chapter 4.

Verify Exposure and Composition

Next, verify the picture on the camera's liquid crystal display, or LCD to ensure that the exposure and composition are acceptable. If the picture is too light (overexposed), too dark (underexposed), or has highlight areas with no detail, adjust the exposure using exposure compensation. As you review the image in your LCD, look for distracting background elements, closed eyes, and other elements that you can improve. If necessary, retake the picture.

Use the LCD

The camera's LCD provides too small of a view to know if a picture is good or not. If possible zoom the LCD display to get a better idea of the overall quality. Unless the picture is hopelessly flawed, you should not delete it. Instead, wait and evaluate it on your computer.

Transfer Pictures to a Computer

You can transfer pictures from your camera to your computer with a USB cable or docking station. When connected, the camera appears on your computer as a separate drive. You can also transfer pictures with a card reader, a PC Card Adapter, or, with some cameras, a CD. See Chapter 8 to learn more about working with digital image.

FROM START TO FINISH: THE DIGITAL WORKFLOW

Edit Pictures

You can use image-editing software that comes with your camera, computer, or software that you purchase to edit pictures. Image-editing programs enable you to rotate, adjust color and saturation, correct red eye, remove unwanted elements, crop, resize, sharpen, combine, and add text to digital pictures. See Chapters 10 and 11 to learn more about working with image-editing software.

Print and Share Pictures

After you edit, size, and sharpen your pictures, you can print them on a home photo-quality printer, or at a commercial printing service. You can also share them in an e-mail message or on a photo-sharing Web site. For more information on printing and sharing pictures, see Chapters 13, 14, and 15.

Organize and Store Digital Negatives

You should not alter the digital negative, the original digital image from the camera. Instead, always work with a copy, and keep the original file untouched.

To manage your picture collection, you can create folders on your computer to organize pictures by date or event. You can archive older pictures by burning them to a CD or DVD.

Clear the Memory Card

After your pictures are on your computer, you can safely delete pictures from your memory card. To delete pictures, you should look for a menu option such as Format Card.

Digital Ca

MINOLTA 3.2

Kodak
EasyShare

ZOOM NIKKOR

CD-RW
REWRITABLE CD
700 MB/80MIN

REUSABLE

Dependable, low-cost media
for archive backup

CD

Archival and tempo...

2X to 48X speed

DVD-R
RECORDABLE DVD

Perfect for storing:
• Music Collections
• Archive files
• Movies

4.7
GB

DVD

Sale Price
$299 00

PictureFix

FREE
with camera purchase

PictureFix

Lite Edition
Image-Editing
Program

CHAPTER 2

What You Need to Get Started

Knowing the basics about digital cameras, resolution, lenses, batteries, and accessories helps you choose the camera that is right for you. Having a digital darkroom enables you to edit and then print your images.

CHOOSE A DIGITAL CAMERA

When choosing a digital camera, consider the size camera, the resolution, how much control you want to have over the camera settings, the quality and focal range of the lens, the shooting modes you use most often, the life of the battery, and the type of storage media available.

Compact

Compact, or point-and-shoot, digital cameras typically capture photos with image resolutions ranging from 1 to 5 megapixels (millions of pixels). They include a built-in flash and a variety of scene modes. Compact cameras offer few, if any, manual controls.

Advanced Non-SLR

Advanced non-SLR (single-lens reflex) digital camera resolution ranges from 4 to 5 megapixels. These cameras feature more exposure control than compact cameras. Some offer wide-angle and telephoto accessory lenses.

Digital SLR

Resolutions for a digital SLR camera range from 4 to 14 megapixels. These cameras offer all of the features and controls found on film SLR cameras. Prices for digital SLRs do not include a lens, and many cameras do not include a pop-up flash.

Lens Considerations

Most compact cameras come with a 3X lens in the 38mm to 105mm range. To get sharp images, look for a high-quality glass lens made by a reputable manufacturer. Ensure that the lens has a "fast" aperture of f/2.8 or faster. Also look for lenses designated as aspherical and low dispersion to help avoid lens distortions and aberrations. You can learn more about lenses in Chapter 4.

Evaluate Exposure and Scene Modes

As a baseline, look for a camera that includes automatic and semi-automatic exposure modes. Most compact cameras include scene modes that automatically set the camera's focal length, shutter speed, and flash based on the scene mode that you choose. Advanced non-SLR cameras include semi-automatic and manual controls, and some also include scene modes.

Batteries

Depending on the model, digital cameras use disposable, rechargeable, or product-specific batteries. Some cameras can use disposable and rechargeable batteries interchangeably. This is convenient because you can use disposable batteries when you cannot recharge batteries and use rechargeable batteries other times. Always buy the right type of battery, and get at least two sets of batteries to ensure uninterrupted shooting.

Storage Media

Digital cameras store pictures on removable memory media, such as a memory card, memory stick, CD, or microdrive. Storage media, commonly referred to as memory cards, comes in a variety of sizes. The size you need depends on the resolution of your camera, and the type you need depends on the camera you buy. Most memory cards are sturdy and reusable.

CONSIDER DIGITAL CAMERA ACCESSORIES

Although most digital cameras come with everything you need to take your first pictures, you can add helpful accessories. Accessories include higher-capacity memory cards, a card reader, extra or better batteries, an accessory flash, accessory lenses, and a tripod.

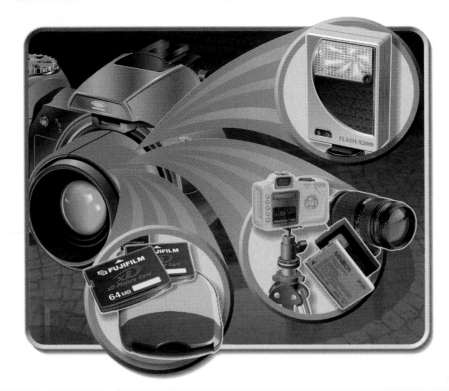

Higher Capacity Memory Cards

Digital cameras come with memory cards ranging in size from 8MB to 32MB, which is fine if you shoot images at low-resolution settings. However, capturing better-quality images requires that you use a high-resolution setting. A higher capacity memory card lets you store more high-resolution images. Which size memory card you need depends on the camera resolution.

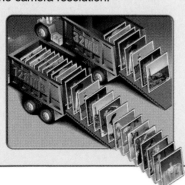

Memory Card Capacity

The number of images a memory card can hold depends on the resolution of the camera and the file format and compression you set using the image-quality menu on the camera. To learn more about image resolution, file formats, and compression, see Chapter 1.

Storage Card Capacity (MB)	Camera Resolution			
	2MP	3MP	4MP	5MP
32	35	26	16	12
64	71	53	32	25
128	142	106	64	51
256	284	213	128	102
512	568	426	256	204

*Numbers are approximate and based on high-resolution camera settings.

Card Readers

You can easily transfer pictures from your camera to your computer using the USB cable, or camera dock. However, a memory card reader provides a continuously connected and convenient way to transfer images. Most card readers connect to the computer using a USB cable, and some card readers accept multiple types of memory cards, such as xD-Picture Cards and SmartMedia.

Accessory Lenses

If your camera accepts interchangeable or accessory lenses, the lenses offer you additional photography flexibility. Look for accessory lenses from the manufacturer of your camera and from aftermarket suppliers. Most accessory lenses require step-up or step-down rings. The ring attaches to the camera's lens, and then the accessory lens attaches to the other side of the ring.

Courtesy Olympus USA

Accessory Flash Unit

Flash

If your camera has a flash mount, or *hot shoe,* you can add a versatile accessory flash unit. If your camera does not have a hot shoe, you can use a flash unit called a *slave* that does not attach to your camera. The built-in flash of the camera triggers the slave unit. To learn more about lighting and flash photography, see Chapter 3.

Reflectors

You can redirect or add light to your subject by using a reflector. You can use the reflector to add light to dark areas and to eliminate harsh shadows on the subject. Reflectors come in many shapes, sizes, and reflective colors. See Chapter 3 to learn more about controlling light with reflectors.

CONSIDER DIGITAL CAMERA ACCESSORIES

Tripods

You can take sharp pictures in lower light scenes if your camera is absolutely stable and if the subject does not move. You can stabilize your camera by using a tripod. Tripods range from small tabletop versions, which are suitable for small digital cameras, to full-size tripods suitable for large digital cameras. Look for a solid, well-built, tripod.

Camera and Accessory Bag

Also consider buying a weather-resistant camera bag. Bags range in size from small pouches to full-size bags with compartments for flash units, lenses, and spare batteries.

To protect easy-to-loose memory cards, you can buy hard- or soft-sided memory card cases that hold two or more memory cards.

No Filter

Polarizing Filter

Filters

Although digital cameras don't require color correction filters, some traditional filters including a *UV filter* can protect the lens of some digital cameras. You can also use a *polarizing* filter on some digital cameras to reduce reflections and to make colors more vibrant.

Creative Filters

You can use filters to add starbursts and halo effects to lights. A *diffuser* filter creates a light fog effect by using a soft focus. Color filters alter the color of your picture. You can also reproduce the effects of some creative filters in most image-editing software.

Cleaning Supplies

To clean your lens, you can use microfiber lens-cleaning cloths and a blower brush. You can also use a *lens pen*. A lens pen has a brush on one end to sweep away particles, and a circular pad with lens-cleaning fluid to wipe away smudges on the other end.

BUILD A DIGITAL DARKROOM

With a digital darkroom, you can ensure that your pictures have great color and contrast and that they are precisely cropped. To create a digital darkroom, you need a computer, monitor, and software for editing images.

Computer

Digital photo files and photo editing tasks require more hard drive space and RAM than text files and processing requires. To speed up digital photography work, it's helpful to have a computer with sufficient RAM, a hard drive with free space to store photos, and a reasonably large monitor that you can calibrate for accurate color.

Minimum System Requirements

A good way to determine if your computer RAM and hard disk space are adequate for image editing is to check the system requirements for both the image-editing program and the operating system. You can find this information are on the side of the software product box.

CD or DVD Archiving

As your digital image collection grows, it is a good practice to archive images on CDs or DVDs. A recordable CD stores 650MB at a cost of 25 cents or less per CD. A recordable DVD stores 4.7GB of data. DVD prices vary by brand and DVD format, but they cost significantly more than CDs. You can also consider using a Jaz or Zip drive for long-term storage.

Recordable CD and DVD Media

A *CD-R* or a *DVD-R, DVD+R* disc allows you to write to the CD once and read from the CD/DVD repeatedly. A *CD-R, DVD+RW, DVD-RW, or DVD-RAM* disc allows you to write to, erase, and read from the CD/DVD repeatedly, much like a floppy disk. CD-R and DVD-R discs are less expensive than CD-RW and DVD rewritable discs, but they cannot be reused.

Choose an Image-Editing Program

An image-editing program allows you to adjust the contrast and color, and to rotate, crop, and add text and special effects to your pictures taken in JPEG or TIFF format. If you take photos in *RAW*, unprocessed, format, you must use a RAW converter program to view, edit, and convert the images to JPEG or TIFF format. You can then further edit the images using any image-editing program.

Monitor Types, Sizes, and Settings

Both CRTs and flat-panel display digital images accurately. A 15-inch computer monitor is adequate, but a 17-inch or larger monitor provides additional photo viewing space. Screen resolution on a 15-inch monitor should be at least 800 x 600 pixels, and, on a 17-inch monitor, it should be at least 1024 x 768 pixels. Set the color to 16 bits, preferably 24 or 32 bits depending on your graphics adapter.

CHOOSE A PHOTO PRINTER

High-quality, affordable photo printers along with premium photo paper enable you to easily print your own photos. You can choose from a variety of printers that can produce long-lasting prints.

Inkjet Printers

Inkjet printers, the most common printer type, use four or more ink colors. They spray tiny droplets of colored ink (usually organic dyes) onto the paper to print the photo. Depending on the quality of the ink and paper, inkjet prints can last from several months to many years without fading.

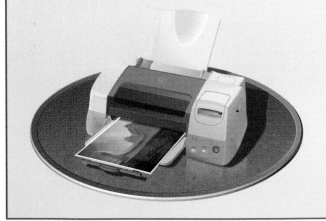

Dye-Sublimation Printers

Dye-sublimation, or *dye-sub,* printers apply heat to a printer ribbon producing a colored gas that dries to create the photo. Dye-sub printers produce continuous-tone prints that most closely resemble traditional film prints, and the print life is comparable to high-quality inkjet prints.

Print Directly from Memory Media

Direct printing lets you print pictures without transferring pictures to your computer first. On some printers, you can insert the memory card into a slot, and then print all or some of the images. On direct-print printers, you can attach your digital camera to the printer using a USB cable, and then print all or part of the images.

Printing Speed

Usually the printing speed published by the manufacturer is for draft quality printing, and not for the best photo quality printing. Print speed is measured in pages per minute (PPM).

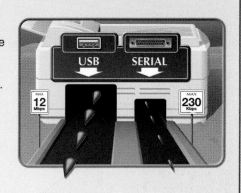

Paper Size

Printers commonly use 8.5" x 11" paper to print an 8" x 10.5" image. Some printers can print on 11" x 14" paper and larger paper sizes.

Connection

Printers connect to the computer using a serial or USB cable. A USB cable provides a faster connection than a serial cable.

Cost

The manufacturer cost-per-print estimates are usually not figured at the best setting of the printer, which uses more ink. You should use manufacturer estimates for comparison only. Color print costs range from approximately 18 cents to $2 or more per 8" x 10" print.

Print Quality

New inkjet printers usually offer a maximum color resolution of 4800 x 1200 dots per inch (dpi). When you evaluate printed samples from different printers, look for smooth, continuous tones, fine gradations of color, and color accuracy and fidelity.

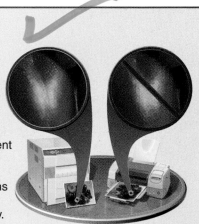

CHAPTER 3

Understanding Light

Learn how to use light to create a mood or atmosphere, define a shape or a form, and bring out details in your photographs.

LEARN ABOUT THE COLOR OF LIGHT

You can use the qualities of light to set the mood and to control a viewer's emotional response to the picture. You can also use light to reveal or subdue the subject's shape, form, texture, and detail, and to show colors in the scene as vibrant or subdued.

Light and Color

All visible light is found within the color spectrum. You see the color more at sunrise and sunset when the sun's low angle causes light to pass through more of the earth's atmosphere. But even midday light has color, as does indoor light, candlelight, and electronic flashes.

Sunrise

Cobalt and purple hues of the night sky predominate during early sunrise. Within minutes, the landscape begins to reflect the warm gold and red hues of the low-angled sun as it comes over the horizon. Then the light shifts to a rich blue. In these minutes, light enhances the green colors of foliage, and earth tones take on a cool hue.

Midday

During midday, the warm and cool colors of light equalize to create a white or neutral light. Although bright midday light is too harsh for some types of photography, particularly portraiture, midday light works well for photographing shadow patterns, flower petals and plant leaves made translucent against the sun, and for natural and manmade structures such as rock formations and buildings.

Sunset

During the time just before, during, and just following sunset, the warmest and most intense color of natural light occurs. The predominantly red, yellow, and gold light creates vibrant colors, while the low angle of the sun creates soft contrasts that define and enhance textures and shapes. Sunset colors create rich landscape, cityscape, and wildlife photographs.

Electronic Flash

Most on-camera electronic flashes are balanced for the neutral (white) color of midday light, while others are balanced toward the cool end of the color spectrum. Electronic flash light is neutral, and in the correct intensities, reproduces colors accurately. However, direct flash often produces hard shadows behind the subject as shown here.

Household Light

Tungsten is household light. Tungsten light is warmer than daylight and produces a yellow/orange cast in photos taken using a digital camera that has the white balance set to daylight or auto.

Fluorescent Light

Commonly found in office and public places, fluorescent light ranges from a yellow to a blue-green hue. Fluorescent light produces a green cast in photos taken using a digital camera that has the white balance set to daylight or auto.

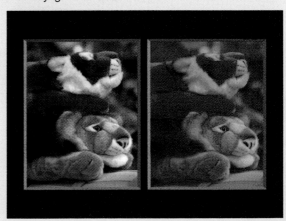

MEASURING AND FILTERING FOR LIGHT

In film photography, you can attach color filters to the lens to compensate for or enhance various light colors. But in digital photography, setting the white balance modifies color temperature.

How Light Color Is Measured

In photography, image color is based on light temperature. Each color of light corresponds to a temperature measured on the Kelvin (K) scale in degrees. The higher the temperature, the cooler (or more blue) the light. The lower the temperature, the warmer (or more yellow/red) the light.

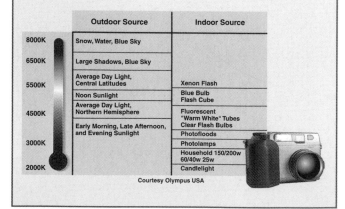

	Outdoor Source	Indoor Source
8000K	Snow, Water, Blue Sky	
6500K	Large Shadows, Blue Sky	
5500K	Average Day Light, Central Latitudes	Xenon Flash
	Noon Sunlight	Blue Bulb Flash Cube
4500K	Average Day Light, Northern Hemisphere	Fluorescent "Warm White" Tubes Clear Flash Bulbs
	Early Morning, Late Afternoon, and Evening Sunlight	Photofloods
3000K		Photolamps
		Household 150/200w 60/40w 25w
2000K		Candlelight

Courtesy Olympus USA

Light Meters

Most camera meters assume that everything you focus on is neutral gray, as shown in these gray cards, which reflects 18 percent of the light and absorbs the rest. When a camera meter evaluates a scene, it expects an average balance of dark and light tones, or an average of 18 percent gray. If the scene is average, the exposure is good. If the scene contains large areas of light or dark, the exposure is thrown off.

How Gray Relates to Color

The light and dark values of color correspond to the tonal continuum of grays along the grayscale. A light shade of red, for example, has a corresponding shade of gray on a grayscale. The lighter the color's shade, the more light it reflects.

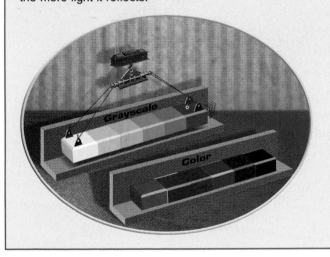

Why Filter for Light?

The human eye automatically adjusts to changing light color and sees white as being white in different types of light. Cameras do not adjust to light changes as the human eye does. To produce accurate color in pictures, digital cameras (and film) need to know the light temperature in the scene. Otherwise, pictures exhibit off-color overall hues such as green or yellow/orange.

White Balance

You tell a digital cameras what the kind of light is in the scene by setting white balance. Digital cameras set to automatic or daylight white balance reproduce colors in a scene accurately at 5,500 to 6,000 degrees K — the light temperature at noon on a cloudless day. The camera's color accuracy decreases as the light temperature moves higher or lower on the Kelvin scale.

Set White Balance

On digital cameras, you adjust the white balance to tell the camera the temperature or type of light in the scene. White balance options, such as Bright Sun, Tungsten, and Fluorescent, are set using one of the camera menus. Choose the setting that matches the predominant light in the scene. Some cameras allow you to adjust setting with a + or – to get more precise color.

PHOTOGRAPH IN VARIED LIGHTING

Photographers describe light as harsh or soft. Harsh light creates shadows with well-defined edges. Soft light creates shadows with soft edges. Understanding the effect of each type of light helps you use both types of light, and the variations between them, effectively.

Harsh Light

Hard light creates a concentrated spotlight effect. Harsh light from the bright sun, a flash, or a bare light bulb creates shadows with sharp edges, and obliterates highlight and shadow details. Use hard light for photographing strong textures, shapes, and bold colors. For other subjects, use a fill flash, move to a shady area, or use a diffusion panel between the light and the subject.

Soft Light

Soft light is diffused light that is spread over a larger area. Atmospheric conditions such as clouds diffuse natural light, creating shadow edges that transition gradually. Soft light works well for portraits and close-up photography. To create separation between the subject and background, use a telephoto lens as shown here. When shooting travel and landscape photography in soft light, look for strong details and bold colors, and avoid including the sky in the photo.

Front Lighting

Front lighting strikes the subject straight on. This type of lighting produces a flat, one-dimensional effect with little texture detail, and with shadows behind the subject. To work with this light, add light to the side of the subject to create depth if possible, or move the subject to a different location.

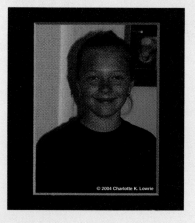

Side Lighting

Side lighting places the light to the side of and at the same height as the subject. This lighting shows one side of the subject brightly lit, and the other side in deep shadow. Side lighting works well for rugged, angular portraits of men but many consider it too harsh for portraits of women.

Top Lighting

Top lighting illuminates the subject from overhead, such as what happens at noon on a sunny, cloudless day. This lighting produces strong, deep shadows, especially under the eyes, nose, and chin. While this lighting direction works for some subjects, for other subjects, you can use fill-flash to add light to the shadow areas.

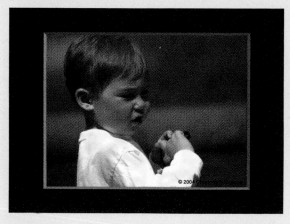

Back Lighting

Light positioned behind the subject creates backlighting. This type of light at normal exposures creates a silhouette, and depending on the angle, can also display a thin halo of light that outlines the shape of the subject. If you do not want the subject to be shown as a silhouette, you can use the fill flash option on your camera.

USING A FLASH

When you need to add light in a low-light scene or in bright top lighting, use the camera's built-in flash unit or an external unit.

Flash Distance

To get the best flash pictures, indoors or outdoors, it is important to know the distance that the flash travels, and then to stay within that distance when taking pictures. On most compact cameras, the flash range is 10 to 15 feet. Be sure to check your camera manual to find the exact range of your flash.

Flash Compensation

Some digital cameras and accessory flash units allow you to reduce flash intensity. You can set the flash between -0.5 and -1 Exposure Values to decrease the flash output to create a softer light. If your flash does not offer compensation, you can place a facial tissue over the flash to reduce the intensity.

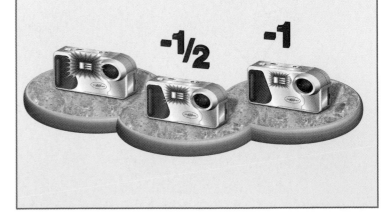

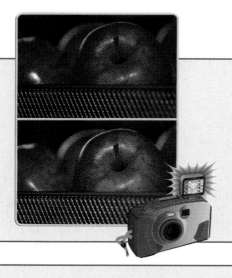

Use Flash Outdoors

You can use your camera's built-in flash outdoors to add light to pictures of people and still life subjects that are at least five feet away. Using flash in overcast and shady scenes often adds a noticeable color and increased contrast to images. Here, fill flash increased the color and brightness of a basket of apples sitting on a shelf in the shade.

Without Fill Flash

Harsh overhead (top) lighting and backlighting create problems, such as unattractive shadows in portraits, and silhouettes. In this picture, without a fill flash, deep shadows appear under the nose and chin of the subject.

With Fill Flash

In this picture, fill flash lightens the deep shadow areas by adding light to the front of the subject.

CHAPTER 4

Control Exposure and Focal Length

From aperture to shutter speed to focal length, you can mix and match camera settings to gain creative control over your pictures. All you need is an understanding of the basic elements of photography.

LEARN ABOUT ISO

Similar to film speeds, ISO settings on digital cameras indicate the digital image sensor's speed, or sensitivity to light.

ISO=FILM SPEED

The higher the ISO setting, the more sensitive the film or sensor is to light, and the less light it takes to make a picture. The lower the ISO setting, the less sensitive the sensor is to light, and more light it takes to create a picture.

ISO Settings

On most digital cameras, you can choose an ISO using a camera menu. Choosing a faster, or higher, ISO allows you to take pictures in scenes with less light and decreases the chance of getting a blurry photo. On many digital cameras, however, settings over 400 can produce digital *noise,* small multicolor flecks, in the picture. For well-lit scenes, a 125 or 200 ISO works well.

© 2004 Charlotte K. Lowrie

LEARN ABOUT APERTURE

The camera aperture, controlled by a diaphragm mechanism, determines how much or how little the lens opens to let in the light that strikes the image sensor.

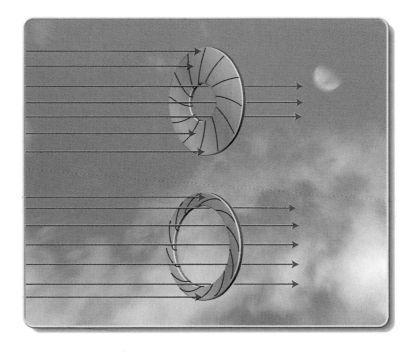

Set the F-Stop

Aperture is shown as f-stop numbers, such as f/2.8, f/4, f/5.6, and f/8. These numbers refer to whether the diaphragm mechanism opens a little or a lot. A wide f-stop, such as f/2.8, allows more light to strike the image sensor. A narrow f-stop, such as f/16, lets in less light.

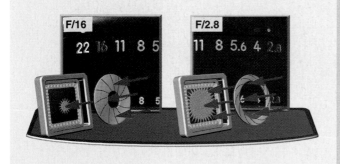

Set the Aperture

If the camera is set to program, automatic, or a scene mode, then the camera automatically sets the aperture. If the camera is set to aperture-priority mode then you can control the aperture by choosing the f-stop on one of the camera's menus or by using the aperture ring or control dial, and the camera automatically sets the correct shutter speed. In manual mode, you choose the aperture and the shutter speed.

CONTROL DEPTH OF FIELD

Depth of field refers to the area in front of and behind a subject that is in acceptably sharp focus. In general, the zone of sharpness extends one-third in front of and two-thirds behind the point you focus on.

Pictures with a soft background show little depth of field, achieved by setting a wide aperture such as f/4 or moving closer to the subject. Pictures with the foreground and much of the background in focus show extensive depth of field, achieved by setting a narrow aperture, such as f/11 or moving farther from the subject.

Adjust the Aperture

To increase the depth of field in a photo where you want as much of the scene in reasonably sharp focus as possible, choose a narrow aperture such as f/8 or f/11. To decrease the depth of field in a photo where you want the background to be out of focus, choose a wider aperture such as f/2.8, f/4, or f/5.6.

Change the Camera-to-Subject Distance

Regardless of the f-stop you choose, the farther away you are from a subject, the greater the depth of field. As you move closer to the subject, the zone of acceptable focus, or depth of field, narrows.

Change Lens Focal Length

Focal length determines how much of a scene the lens "sees." A wide-angle lens or zoom setting sees more of the scene than a telephoto lens or zoom setting sees. A wide-angle lens or zoom setting provides more depth of field than a telephoto lens or zoom setting, if you are not extremely close to the subject.

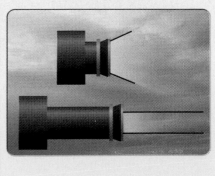

Shutter speed controls how long the *curtain,* a mechanism that covers the sensor, stays open to let light from the lens strike the image sensor. The longer the shutter stays open, the more light reaches the sensor, at the aperture you set.

Shutter speeds, shown in fractions of a second, range from slow, 1 second, 1/2, 1/4, 1/8, 1/15, 1/30, 1/60 sec., to fast, 1/125, 1/500, 1/1000 sec. Increasing or decreasing the shutter speed by one setting halves or doubles the exposure respectively.

Set the Shutter Speed

On fully automatic cameras, or in program or scene mode on other cameras, the camera sets the shutter speed. For example, in Sports scene mode, the camera selects a fast shutter speed to freeze subject motion. In semi-automatic modes, you can set the shutter speed using one of the camera's menus.

Freeze or Blur Subject Motion

To freeze motion in normal scenes, set the shutter speed to 1/60 sec. or faster. To blur motion as a blur, use 1/30 sec. or slower, and mount the camera on a tripod. At a slow shutter speed, such as 1/30 sec., you can follow subject movement with the camera and blur the background as shown here. This technique is called a *pan-blur*.

© 2004 Charlotte K. Lowrie

DISCOVER EXPOSURE MODES

Selecting an exposure mode gives you a little or a lot of control over what exposures you can choose and how your pictures look. Semi-automatic modes give you more creative control over depth of field and whether you freeze or blur motion.

Auto Mode

Auto mode, sometimes called Program mode, works well when you want to just point and shoot. In this mode, the camera selects the aperture, or f-stop, and shutter speed for the correct exposure. Although Auto mode is not the most creative way to use your camera, it works well when you want to quickly capture a picture.

Aperture-Priority Mode

You can use aperture-priority mode, when you want to choose the aperture, or f-stop, and have the camera automatically set the shutter speed. Aperture-priority mode works well when you want creative control over depth of field. If you choose a narrow f-stop in a low-light scene, you may need to steady the camera on a tripod due to the slow shutter speed.

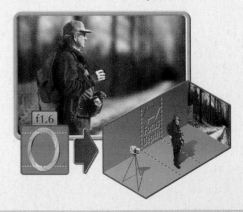

f1.6

Shutter-Priority Mode

You can use shutter-priority mode, when you want to choose the shutter speed and have the camera automatically set the correct aperture, or f-stop. Shutter-priority mode works well when you want to control how action appears. A fast shutter speed freezes action. A slow shutter speed shows motion as a blur.

Subject Modes

You can use a subject or scene mode when you want to the camera to automatically set the exposure based on a specific scene. Common scene modes include sports, landscape, portrait, and close-up. Scene modes work well when you want to point and shoot and use classic exposure settings that are appropriate the scene.

Manual Mode

You can use manual mode, when you want to choose the shutter speed and the aperture. Manual mode works well when you want control over depth of field and the ability to freeze or blur motion. When you change the f-stop or the shutter speed, the camera shows the appropriate setting for the other variable in the viewfinder. Consult your camera manual for specific instructions.

LEARN ABOUT FOCAL LENGTH

Focal length determines the angle of view, or how much of a scene the camera's lens sees. In addition, focal length plays a role in determining the sharpness or softness of the background and foreground objects in a scene or the depth of field.

To learn more about depth of field, see the section "Control Depth of Field."

Focal Length Defined

Focal length determines how much of the scene the lens sees, or the angle of view of the lens. For example, on a 35mm camera, a 17mm lens has a wider angle of view than the human eye can see, encompassing a broad sweep of the scene. A telephoto lens has a much narrower view, and focuses on a single, distant element.

Using a Normal Lens

On a 35mm camera, a 50mm to 55mm lens is considered a normal lens because it sees approximately the same angle of view as the human eye sees. On most digital cameras, a 35mm lens is closer to normal because the image sensor is smaller than a 35mm film frame, which magnifies the view approximately 1.5 times depending on the camera sensor.

USING A WIDE-ANGLE LENS

A wide-angle, or wider than 50mm, lens provides an broad angle of view and extensive depth of field, especially at small apertures, if you are not standing close to the subject. Use a wide-angle lens or zoom setting to photograph landscapes, panoramas, large groups, and for shooting in a small area where you want to capture the entire scene.

© 2004 Charlotte K. Lowrie

Wide-Angle Distortion

Wide-angle lenses distort the relative size and spacing of objects in a scene. For example, objects close to the lens seem larger than they are, while distant objects seem farther away, and farther apart than you remember seeing them. Wide-angle lenses can distort lines particularly if you tilt the camera upward or downward so that lines appear to converge. This effect is called *keystoning*.

Aspherical Lens

An aspherical lens has a non-spherical surface. These lenses help correct optical flaws to produce better edge sharpness and straighter lines. These lenses are also lighter in weight than non-aspherical lenses because they do not need additional lens elements, or additional glass, to correct for edge sharpness.

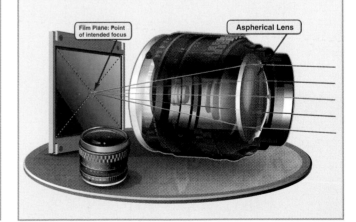

USING A TELEPHOTO LENS

A telephoto, or wider than 50mm, lens provides a narrow angle of view and limited depth of field. You can use a telephoto lens or zoom setting to isolate a subject from the background, bring distant objects closer, and compress objects with the background.

Courtesy Olympus USA

Telephoto Compression

Because telephoto lenses compress perspective, elements in a scene appear closer together than you remember seeing them. You can use this compression to create a layering effect in photos.

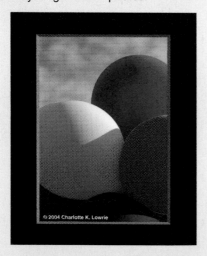

© 2004 Charlotte K. Lowrie

Low-Dispersion Glass

Telephoto lenses and zooms with low-dispersion glass provide increased sharpness, especially at the frame edges, and they provide better color. When you shop for a compact camera or a telephoto lens, look for lenses identified as ED, extra-low dispersion, LD, low dispersion, SLD, super-low dispersion, L, luxury, or APO, apochromatic.

USING A ZOOM LENS

A zoom lens enables you to change the focal length at the touch of a button or by adjusting the zoom ring. A zoom lens combines a range of focal distances within a single lens. Zoom lenses fall within the standard lens categories of wide-angle, for 17mm to 35mm, and telephoto, for 80mm to 200mm.

Courtesy Nikon, Inc.

Choose a Zoom Lens

When you shop for a camera with a zoom lens or a standalone zoom lens, look for lenses with aspherical or low-dispersion glass. When you use a zoom lens, set the lens at f/8 or f/11 to get the best sharpness.

Courtesy Nikon, Inc.

Prevent Blurry Pictures

Zooming in on your subject exaggerates even the slightest camera movement, resulting in blurred images, especially when you take photos at slower shutter speeds. When shooting at slower shutter speeds you can stabilize your camera by mounting it on a tripod.

LEARN ABOUT DIGITAL CAMERA LENSES

Understanding a Multiplication Factor

Digital cameras image sensors smaller than a 35mm film frame reduce the angle of view and produce an apparent lens magnification. Magnification varies by factors ranging from 1.3 to 1.5 times. At 1.5 factor, a 100 — 3 00mm lens provides a 150 — 450mm equivalent angle of view. This gives greater magnification when you photograph distant subjects but gives a narrower view of the scene at wide-angle settings.

Optical Versus Digital Zoom

Many digital cameras offer optical and digital zoom. Optical zoom magnifies the scene by changing the focal length. Digital zoom crops the scene and then magnifies the center of the frame to make the subject appear larger. Some cameras add extra pixels to round out the image size or resolution. This cropping effect often degrades image quality. Always avoid using digital zoom.

Optical Zoom

Digital Zoom

Digital-Specific Lenses

Companies including Olympus, Kodak, and Fujifilm, are developing the *Four-Thirds System* that establishes a new common standard for the interchange of lenses developed for digital SLR cameras. The *Four-Thirds System* allow the development of dedicated digital-camera lens systems. With a sensor measuring half the size of a 35mm film frame, the Four-Thirds System produces a 2x multiplier for the new digital lenses.

Courtesy Olympus USA

What You See versus What the Lens Sees

Many compact digital cameras feature optical viewfinders, but the viewfinders are separate from the lens. As a result, you do not see in the viewfinder exactly what the lens sees. The closer you move to the subject, the greater the difference, or *parallax,* becomes. To get an accurate view of what the lens "sees," you can use the LCD.

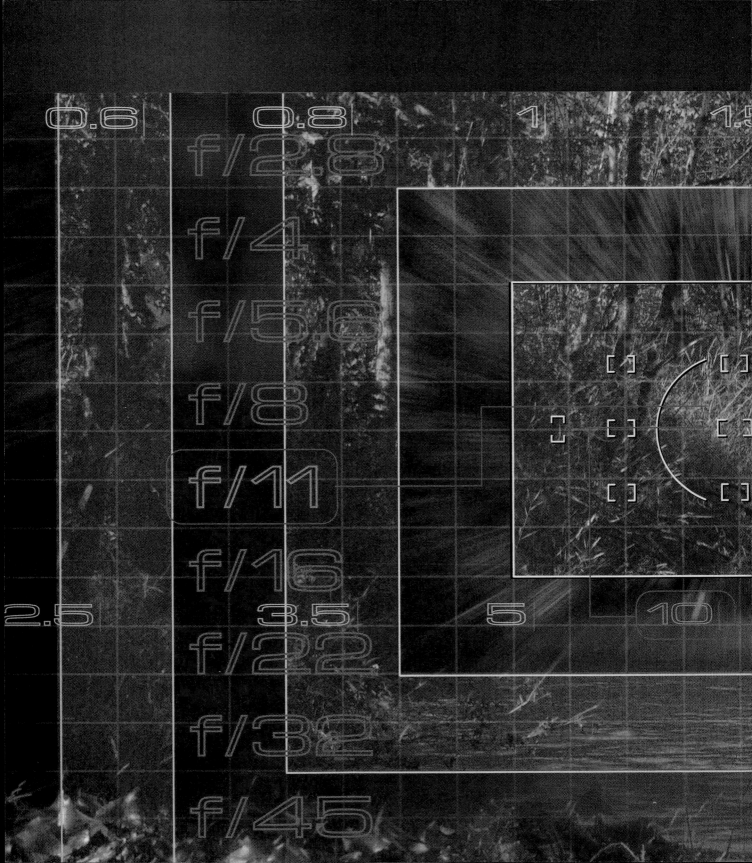

CHAPTER 5

Learn About Focus

Nothing can ruin a picture faster than if the subject is blurry or not in focus. In this chapter, you can learn how to focus precisely and what to focus on in a scene.

Background image © 2004 Charlotte K. Lowrie

UNDERSTANDING FOCUSING SYSTEMS

Automatic focus systems vary from camera to camera. Some cameras use a light to determine focusing distance. Other systems look for differences in the light and dark areas in the scene, and others use sensors.

Fixed Focus Systems

Fixed focus systems do not adjust the lens to focus, but rely only on depth of field to determine focus. While the method is simple, fixed focus systems often display only reasonably sharp pictures. Budget cameras and single-use cameras often use a fixed focus system.

Active Autofocus Systems

Many cameras use active autofocus systems that direct an infrared beam toward the subject. Sensors on the camera detect the light that reflects back. The sensors determine how far away the subject is and use this distance to set the focus.

Passive Autofocus Systems

Some cameras use passive autofocus systems, also called *phase detection*. To determine camera-to-subject distance, the camera detects differences in dark and light elements, or *contrast*, in the scene, or differences in colors and textures. Passive autofocus works well in normal contrast scenes, but does not focus as well in low-light scenes and with little contrast difference, as shown in this picture.

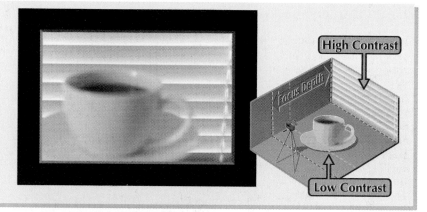

Multipoint Autofocus Systems

Multipoint autofocus systems let you easily compose with and focus on an off-center subject. To focus, you select one of the autofocus sensors, place the subject within the selected sensor, and then focus by pressing the shutter release button halfway down. Some multipoint systems offer focus tracking to maintain continuous focus on a moving subject.

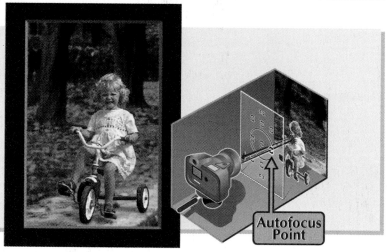

When Autofocus Fails

Autofocus tends to fail when a subject is: a single color, has a regular geometrical pattern, has little or no density, has a reflective or shiny surface, or is moving at high speed.

Autofocus can also fail when the subject is behind glass, is in front of or behind other objects, is distant, dark, or does not reflect light well.

FOCUS ON A STILL SUBJECT

To compose an image with the subject off center, you can use focus lock. In most pictures, you do not want to position the subject in the center of the frame. This makes focusing difficult with cameras that have a single center autofocus sensor.

© 2004 Charlotte K. Lowrie

FOCUS ON A STILL SUBJECT

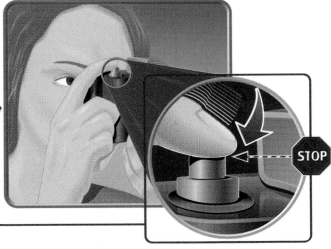

1 Frame your subject in the viewfinder or LCD.

■ Always set the zoom before focusing.

■ For multipoint focusing systems, choose the autofocus sensor you want.

Note: See Chapter 4 to learn about using a zoom lens.

2 Press the shutter release button halfway down.

■ The focus system locks using the center autofocus sensor or the sensor you chose.

3 Check the focus indicator on the camera to ensure the focus is good.

■ Most cameras have a green LED that glows in or near the viewfinder when the subject is in focus.

54

TEACH YOURSELF

Should I compose my pictures using the viewfinder or the LCD?

The LCD provides an accurate view of the scene that the camera captures, whereas the viewfinder may not show the full scene. If you use the LCD to compose pictures, be sure that the focus indicator shows that the focus is good before you take the picture. When you compose using the LCD, consider supporting the camera on a solid surface such as a tripod or a table, or brace yourself against a solid object to ensure that you get sharp pictures.

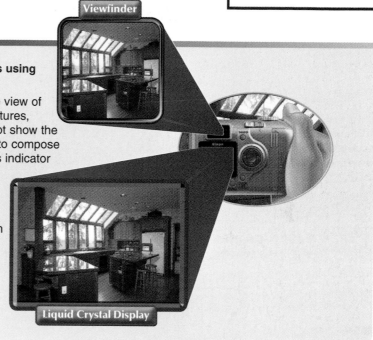

Viewfinder

Liquid Crystal Display

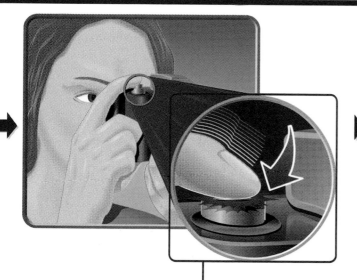

4 If necessary, hold the button halfway down, and then shift the camera to recompose the scene.

5 Fully depress the shutter release button to take the picture.

Note: If you or the subject change position, be sure to repeat this process to refocus on the subject.

■ The camera captures the properly focused picture and saves it to memory.

USING FOCUSING MODES

When you select a subject or scene mode on a compact camera, the camera calculates focus based on the mode you choose.

© 2004 Charlotte K. Lowrie

Check the camera manual to learn the focusing ranges for each mode on your camera.

Automatic

Automatic, or Autofocus, settings usually work well from 1 foot away at a wide zoom setting, to 2 feet away and beyond at a telephoto setting.

Landscape

If you set the camera to Landscape scene mode, then the camera sets the focus at infinity, or the distant elements in the scene.

Portrait

To change the focus for closer distances, switch to Portrait, or Macro, mode.

DISCOVER FOCUS TECHNIQUES

Focus on a Moving Subject

For moving subjects, you can switch to servo, or continuous, focus to track the subject and keep it in focus. Otherwise, you can switch to manual focus, and then focus on a point in the scene to which the subject will move. When the subject reaches that point in the frame, take the picture.

Choose a Point of Focus

When taking a portrait or group picture, focus on the eyes of the person who is closest to the camera. When photographing a still life, focus on the most important element in the scene. For example, in this picture, the focus is on the berries. For a landscape photo, fix the focus one-third of the way into the scene.

Focus Tips

Use a tripod (see Chapter 2).

Shoot at the highest resolution (see Chapter 1).

Use the "sweet spot" of the lens, typically f/8 or f/11.

Avoid using the minimum and maximum apertures of a zoom lens, for example, f/2.8 and f/22.

In dim light, use normal- to wide-angle lenses or zoom settings (see Chapter 4).

CHAPTER 6

Compose Pictures Like a Pro

Want to quickly improve your digital pictures? Improving composition is a quick way to get better pictures. This chapter explores ways to add interest to all your photos using a variety of composition techniques.

THINK ABOUT COMPOSITION

The best pictures not only catch your attention, but they also hold your attention. To get these kinds of pictures, compose images carefully and tell a story in each picture. Begin by borrowing established design principles and composition techniques. As you progress, add in your own personal style to create signature pictures that viewers remember.

© 2004 Charlotte K. Lowrie

Stand Back and Evaluate

You interpret each scene for your viewers. It is your job to combine your emotional perceptions with the objective viewpoint of the camera. Begin by evaluating all of the elements in the scene. Gradually narrow your view to identify individual vignettes. Then, look for defining elements, colors, patterns, and textures that can help organize the visual information in the picture.

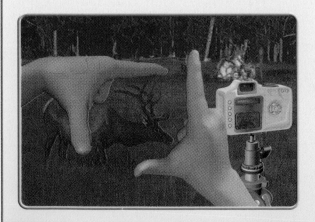

Consider Audience and Occasion

The most important questions to ask during this stage are "Why am I taking this picture?" and "What do I want to tell the viewer?" Answering these questions helps you focus on the important elements in the scene. From there, you can choose to include or exclude visual elements that add to or detract from the message you want to communicate to viewers.

Use Light and Exposure Controls Creatively

Once you know the message you want to convey, you can use or modify the light, and choose exposure settings that create the mood, concentrate attention, and provide the perspective of the scene. In this picture, backlighting against a blue sky, emphasizes the grace and hopefulness that the rose symbolizes. To learn more about light, see Chapter 3. To learn more about exposure, see Chapter 4.

© 2004 Charlotte K. Lowrie

© 2004 Charlotte K. Lowrie

Keep It Simple

Just as with writing or painting, messages are most effectively delivered and retained when they are simple. Strive for a clean shot — an uncluttered visual scene that conveys a single story, or conveys a clear graphic shape, as shown here. To get a clean shot, you can clear away clutter, change your shooting position, or zoom in on the subject.

Evaluate the Result

With a digital camera, you can immediately evaluate the success or failure of your images on the LCD. Take advantage of the opportunity to make adjustments, and immediately reshoot the picture. The more pictures that you take and edit, the better you become at recognizing problems by looking at pictures on the LCD.

CONSIDER DESIGN PRINCIPLES

Many principles of photographic composition are influenced by the traditional design disciplines of art and graphic design. Here are a few of the most widely used principles.

Is Symmetry Good or Bad?

Perfectly symmetrical compositions, images that are the same from side to side or from top to bottom, create balance and stability, but they also are viewed as boring compositions. Symmetrical designs often offer less visual impact than photos with some asymmetry and tension, as shown here.

Create a Sense of Balance

Balance is a sense of "rightness" in a photo. A balanced photo does not appear to be too heavy at any point, or too off center. When composing your pictures, consider the following: the visual weight of colors and tones — dark is heavier than light; objects — large objects appear heavier than small objects; and placement — objects placed toward an edge appear heavier than objects placed at the center of the frame.

What Lines Convey

Lines have symbolic significance that you can use to direct the focus and organize the visual elements in your picture. Horizontal lines imply stability and peacefulness. Diagonal lines imply strength, as shown in this picture, and dynamic tension. Vertical lines imply motion, while curved lines symbolize grace, and zigzag lines imply action.

How the Shapes of Objects Affect Photos

The number and kind of shapes in a photo determine where viewers focus their attention. The human shape or form always draws attention in a picture. A single, small shape attracts attention either as the subject or as a secondary element that helps to define the subject. Groupings of similar objects invite the viewer to compare size, shape, and spacing between the objects.

Placement of a Subject within a Picture

Just as symmetry is visually uninteresting, placing a subject or the line of the horizon in the center of the frame is usually equally boring. Subject placement depends on the scene, but placement should identify the subject, and create a natural visual path through the photo. Also, motion and implied action should come into the frame rather than travel out of it.

PRACTICE TRADITIONAL COMPOSITION TECHNIQUES

Many established techniques can improve your photos. While there are no binding rules of composition, the techniques in this section provide a good starting point for designing images. Be sure to experiment and let the subject help define the composition.

© 2004 Charlotte K. Lowrie

Choose the Orientation

The most basic composition begins by choosing either a horizontal or a vertical orientation. Some subjects dictate the most appropriate orientation. For example, you can use a horizontal orientation for a sweeping landscape, and a vertical orientation for a portrait, as shown in this picture. Otherwise, choose the orientation that supports the composition you envision and avoids useless, empty space.

Fill the Frame

Just as an arti fills an entire canvas with a scene, photographers strive to fill the image frame with elements that support the message. Decide exactly what you want in the picture, and then fill the frame with what you choose for the picture. For variation, you can come in very close to the subject to show only part of the subject.

Check the Background and Surroundings

In a picture, the elements behind and around the subject become as much a part of the photograph as the subject. As you compose the picture, check everything in the viewfinder or LCD for objects that compete with or distract from the subject. Then see if you can move the objects, the subject, or change your position, as shown here, to eliminate distractions.

Practice the Rule of Thirds

A popular photography compositional technique draws an imaginary grid over the viewfinder. With the scene divided into thirds, the photographer places the subject on one of the points of intersection or along one of the lines on the grid. In a portrait, you can place the eyes of the subject at the upper-left intersection point, which is considered to be the strongest position.

Frame the Subject

Photographers often borrow a technique from painters, putting the subject within a naturally occurring frame, such as a tree framed by a barn door, or a distant building framed by an archway in the foreground. The frame may or may not be in focus, but for it to be most effective, it should add context to the subject.

Use Other Composition Aids

Other composition techniques include using strong textures, repeating patterns and geometric shapes, and color repetition or contrasts to compose images. These elements can create a picture on their own, or you can use them to create visual motion that directs the eye or supports the subject.

WAYS TO CONTROL COMPOSITION

In a perfect world, you could control all of the elements within a photograph. In the real world, you work with existing scenes. Here are some ways to get the best composition when you cannot control all of the elements in the scene.

© 2004 Charlotte K. Lowrie

Select Focus and Control Depth of Field

Because the eye is drawn to the sharpest part of the photo, you can use focus to emphasize the relative importance of elements in the picture. Or combine selective focus and depth of field to emphasize or subdue elements within the picture. Here, a shallow depth of field blurs a distracting background. For more information on depth of field, see Chapter 4.

© 2004 Charlotte K. Lowrie

Change the Point of View

Instead of photographing at eye-level, try changing your viewpoint. For instance, if you photograph a subject from a lower-than-eye-level position, then the subject seems powerful, while a higher-than-eye-level position creates the opposite effect.

Use Tone and Contrast

You can use *contrast,* or the difference between light and dark tones, to emphasize your subject. Experiment by modifying the amount and angle of light to create more or less contrast. Or you can change position so the subject is backlit to add dramatic contrast.

Define Space and Perspective

Some techniques to control the perception of space in pictures include changing the distance from the camera to the subject, selecting a telephoto or wide-angle lens or zoom setting, changing the position of the light, and changing the point of view. In this example, a telephoto lens compresses the sense of space.

NIGHT PHOTOGRAPHY

NATURAL LIGHT

SHOW ACTION

DEPTH OF FIELD

CHAPTER 7

Put It All Together

In this chapter, you can practice and see the results of using different exposure factors, lenses or zoom settings, lighting, and scene modes.

EXPERIMENT WITH DEPTH OF FIELD

When you control the depth of field in a picture, you control how much of the scene is in focus. You can use depth of field to guide the attention of the viewer and to create artistic effects.

Control Viewer Focus

To control the depth of field, you can use aperture, focal length, and camera-to-subject distance, individually or in combination. Even at a narrow aperture of f/8, a close camera-to-subject distance creates a shallow depth of field that focuses attention on the foreground tulip.

Limits to Control

Sometimes you cannot use the aperture you want to because of light or technical limitations. In this picture, the bright afternoon sunlight did not allow the use of a wide aperture to limit depth of field. An alternative would be to move closer to the subject. This would decrease depth of field and single out the pumpkin from the background.

Get the Effect You Want

The pictures on this page show how narrow, mid-range, and wide apertures, affect the depth of field, or the zone of sharpness from front to back, in a picture. In this picture, a 19mm setting on a wide-angle zoom lens and a narrow aperture of f/22 create sharp details, or a wide depth of field.

Focus on the Subject

In this picture, an 85mm lens and a wide aperture of f/1.4 gently blur the background and bring the eye of the viewer to the subject in the zone of sharpness.

Classic Landscape and Portrait Apertures

For landscape pictures, use a narrow aperture to create extensive depth of field. For portraits, use a wide aperture to decrease the depth of field. In the picture on the left, a 35mm lens with an aperture of f/22 creates sharp, background detail that distracts from the subject. On the right, a 35mm lens with an aperture of f/2.8 creates a blurry background.

71

EXPERIMENT WITH DEPTH OF FIELD

Use Focal Length for Effect

Focal length also increases or decreases the depth of field. Pictures on this page show how changes in focal length affect the depth of field. In this picture, a 60mm lens at f/8 creates a moderate depth of field. See Chapter 5 for a definition of focal length.

Show the Overall Scene

In this picture, an 80mm lens, at f/11, renders the scene with good front-to-back sharpness. Stopping down to f/22 further increases the depth of field. An 80mm, or moderate telephoto, 50 to 55mm, or normal, or 17 to 35mm, or wide-angle lens or zoom setting works well when you want to show the overall scene.

Show the Scene Details

A longer focal length decreases depth of field and isolates specific areas of the scene. In this picture, a 200mm telephoto lens at f/11 creates a narrow depth of field but provides a more intimate look at the building. You can use a telephoto lens when you cannot physically move closer or when you want to isolate details in a scene.

Move in or Step Back

If you want greater depth of field, but the light or focal length are limited, you can change your position to isolate details or show more of the scene. Pictures on this page show how camera-to-subject distance increases or decreases the depth of field and changes the picture. Here, a close shooting distance with a 60mm lens creates a very shallow depth of field.

© 2004 Charlotte K. Lowrie

© 2004 Charlotte K. Lowrie

Move in Close

In this picture, a 60mm lens at a close distance gives a limited depth of field but shows fine details of the subject. To increase the depth of field, you can move in close, but use a wide-angle lens or zoom setting.

Move Back

The farther you move back, the greater the depth of field becomes, as shown here. Moving back only a few steps can make a significant difference in the depth of field.

© 2004 Charlotte K. Lowrie

MIX AND MATCH SETTINGS

Now that you know how aperture, focal length, and camera-to-subject distance affects pictures, you can combine one, two, or all three factors to create different effects or to find an acceptable exposure in difficult scenes.

Maximize Overall Sharpness

For maximum detail from front to back in a picture, use a wide-angle lens or zoom setting, a narrow aperture, and then move back from the subject. This combination works when you want to take a sweeping landscape picture, or when you are in a confined space and you want to include the entire area.

Maximize Sharpness Up Close

You can combine a wide-angle lens, a narrow aperture, and a close camera-to-subject distance to get acceptable sharpness up close. The wide-angle lens or zoom setting, combined with a narrow aperture, provides a wide depth of field from front to back, despite a close distance.

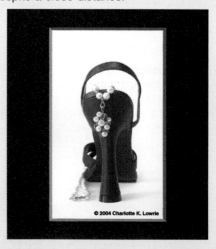

Get a Limited Area of Sharpness

You can combine a telephoto lens, a wider aperture, and a closer camera-to-subject distance for the ideal portrait setting. If you want to emphasize a detail of the subject, then you can move closer to the subject.

Get Maximum Sharpness in Extreme Close-ups

You can combine a telephoto lens, a narrow aperture, and a close camera-to-subject distance when you want to photograph close-up photos, known as *macro* pictures. Because the working distance is close, you can get better depth of field by choosing a narrow aperture. Be sure to use a tripod to ensure a sharp picture.

Get Sharp Everyday Pictures

For everyday shooting, you can combine a normal lens and moderate aperture, such as f/8 or f/11, at any distance to get great results with good sharpness. Consider f/5.6 a point of departure at which the background begins to blur.

USE DIFFERENT SHUTTER SPEEDS FOR EFFECT

You can use shutter speed to stop action or to show action or motion as a blur. You can also experiment with shutter speeds to create unexpected and interesting results.

Stop the Action

You can stop action at shutter speeds faster than 1/30 sec. Faster shutter speeds work well for capturing an athlete in mid-air, or showing subtle action, such as this spinning top that looks as if it is standing still.

Show the Action

At 1/30 sec. and slower shutter speeds, you can show action as a blur, as in this picture. Use slower shutter speeds to capture light trails created by passing traffic at dusk, or for creative light compositions.

© 2004 Charlotte K. Lowrie

FOCUS SELECTIVELY

You can use focus as a way to direct the attention of the viewer to the most important or a single element in a picture. In close-ups, you can switch to manual focus to get the best focus.

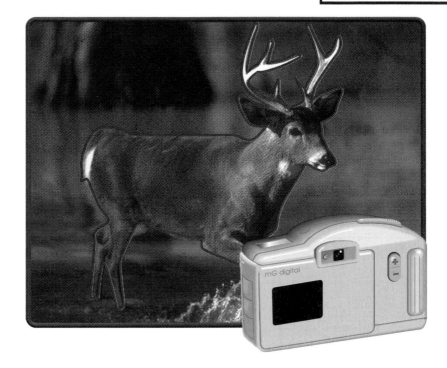

Combine Selective Focus with Distance

To show a small area with fine detail, use a selective focus. In this picture, a narrow aperture of f/32 and sharp focus emphasize the fine details of the rose. In macro pictures, you can switch to manual focus to ensure the sharpest focus.

© 2004 Charlotte K. Lowrie

Combine Selective Focus, Focal Length, and Aperture

When you combine a wide aperture setting with a telephoto lens, and focus carefully, you can narrow the focus even more. As shown in this picture, a telephoto lens and an aperture of f/4.5 create a very specific focus.

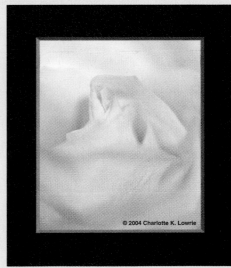

© 2004 Charlotte K. Lowrie

COMPOSE CREATIVELY

You can combine exposure, focal length, and composition to take creative pictures that convey a message or tell a story.

Get to the Point

In this image, exposure settings combine with shooting position and the rule of thirds to narrow in on the message from the writing.

Draw the Viewer In

Here the composition and leading lines guide the viewer through the photo toward the eyes of the subject. A narrow aperture creates good detail throughout the image, despite the close camera-to-subject distance.

Capture the Action

In this image, the low light levels necessitated using a wide aperture and, in this case, the exposure shows the blur of some of the motion while it freezes other motion in the scene.

Create Abstract Images

Colorful, late-afternoon light, a slow shutter speed, and a high ISO setting combine to create this abstract, but appealing, picture of an airplane propeller in motion.

Motion Is Good

If you want to show energy and personality, then you can combine a slow shutter speed and wide aperture, as shown here.

EXPERIMENT WITH DIFFERENT LIGHTING OPTIONS

Modifying light not only overcomes common problems in typical scenes, but it can also give pictures a dramatic flair.

Experiment with a Flash

A built-in flash provides the quickest and most convenient way to alter scene lighting. Experiment with the various synch modes, such as slow, front, and rear curtain synchronization. You can use these modes to obtain good exposures at night and to create front or rear light trails of traffic in dimly lit scenes.

© 2004 Charlotte K. Lowrie

Use Fill Flash

Although fill flash works well for portraits, you can use fill flash for other subjects, as well. For example, you can use fill flash outdoors to highlight outdoor colors in nature pictures. For indoor still-life pictures, fill flash creates interesting effects, as shown here.

© 2004 Charlotte K. Lowrie

Use a Reflector

You can use a reflector to catch natural light and reflect it back into a scene. In this picture, a gold-colored reflector adds light to the face of the subject and creates a warm glow. Experiment with the position of the reflector, but avoid adding too much light, or creating hot spots on the subject. You can purchase small, collapsible reflectors at any camera store.

Wait for the Flattering Light

To get the best pictures, you should wait for the best light of the day. Here, the warm light of late afternoon enhances and deepens the color of the roses.

Watch for the Best Light Plays

It is a good habit to always have your camera with you to capture some of the beautiful natural light plays. In this picture, a storm moves in at sunset, displaying a dramatic interaction of light and color.

TRY CREATIVE TECHNIQUES

Once you practice using standard photography techniques, you can use other variations that can be fun and create interesting images.

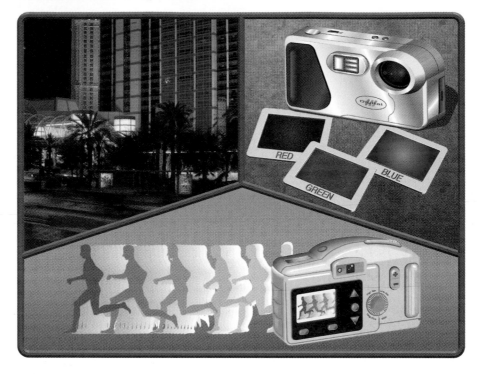

Pan Using a Slow Shutter Speed

At a shutter speed of 1/30 sec. or slower, you can pan with a subject as it moves, making the background appear blurred. To do this, focus on a place where the subject will pass. When the subject enters the viewfinder, follow the subject with the camera, and then take the picture when the subject reaches the point on which you focused.

Use Backlighting

In harsh light, you can sometimes turn the light to your advantage by using it to create silhouettes or to enhance vivid color. To enhance transparent color, take a low shooting position, as shown in this picture.

Capture Light Trails

You can create cool low-light and night images by switching to the low-light or night scene mode. The camera uses a slow shutter speed that captures subjects like moving car lights as streaks of light. If you do not have scene modes, select a shutter speed of 1/30 sec. or slower, use a tripod, and set the self-timer to trip the shutter, avoiding blur from touching the shutter release button.

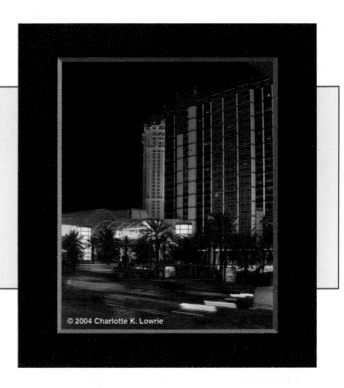

© 2004 Charlotte K. Lowrie

Warm Up Flash Pictures

You can warm up the color of your camera flash by placing colored transparent gels or films over the flash. In the picture on the right, placing a discarded strip of photographic film over the flash adds warmth to the scene, compared to the unfiltered flash picture shown on the left.

© 2004 Charlotte K. Lowrie   © 2004 Charlotte K. Lowrie

CHAPTER 8

Take Your First Digital Pictures

Learn the specifics of setting up a digital camera, and taking, transferring, and evaluating your first set of digital pictures.

SET UP A DIGITAL CAMERA

To get off to a good start with a digital camera, take time to read the manual and to set camera options to ensure that you get the best image quality.

Charge Batteries

As a first step, read the instructions in the quick-start guide or the manual on charging the battery. Some batteries require an overnight charging cycle, while others charge in a few hours. Then insert the fully charged battery in the camera.

Insert the Memory Card

Almost all digital cameras come with a removable memory card, stick, multimedia card, or internal memory. If your memory card has a locking mechanism, unlock the card first. Then locate the slot for the memory card, which often includes a diagram showing the direction that you insert the card. Most cameras do not accept the card if you insert it backwards.

Set the Date and Time

Turn the camera on, and then set it to record or picture-taking mode. Follow the instructions on the LCD to set the date and time. You should set the date and time because they become part of the shooting information that the camera stores with images — information that is helpful for organizing and retrieving images later.

Set the Image Quality and Format

You can set image size, quality, and format on a camera menu. For best quality, set it to the largest size and highest quality. These settings provide the best quality but images require more memory card space. Also choose an image format: JPEG, TIFF, or RAW. *RAW,* a proprietary format that stores images with no in-camera processing, provides powerful post-capture options, but you must use the manufacturer's or third-party software to view and save images.

Set the White Balance

To get accurate color, you can set the white balance to the setting that matches the light in the scene. If you take pictures indoors under household light, set the white balance to tungsten. If you take outdoor pictures, set the white balance to cloudy, shade, or bright daylight, based on the existing scene's light.

TAKE TEST PICTURES

The first pictures you take provide a great baseline for evaluating the performance and characteristics of your camera. Identifying camera characteristics tells you which camera settings to fine-tune to get consistently good pictures.

Learn the Controls

Acquaint yourself with the controls for taking and reviewing images. The mode control dial usually has icons, such as a close-up of a person, mountains, and a movie camera. Locate the zoom control and the control for moving forward and back, to review images and make selections from the camera menus.

Take Pictures

Get started by taking the kinds of pictures you take most often—snapshots of family and friends, indoors and outdoors. Also take pictures with and without the flash, both indoors and outdoors. These pictures establish a baseline, so you can compare them to the results you normally get with film or a previous digital camera.

Adjusting to a Digital Camera

You may need to adjust to slower start-up times, and *shutter lag,* which is the delay between the time you press the shutter-release button and the time the exposure is made. Image recording time depends on the memory card speed: the faster the card speed, the faster the image writes to the card. Never turn off the camera until it records the image to the card, otherwise, you can lose the image.

Compose Shots in the Viewfinder and LCD

For close subjects, use the LCD to compose images. *Parallax* is the slight offset to the right between what you see in the viewfinder and what you get on the image. Parallax becomes more apparent for subjects closer than 3 feet, at maximum zoom settings and 10 feet at telephoto settings. At other distances, you can use the viewfinder to compose images.

Verify Pictures

As you shoot, be sure to check the pictures in the LCD monitor. The LCD is too small to make definitive judgments, but it indicates obvious composition and exposure problems. Most cameras display the picture on the LCD immediately after you take it. To browse through the images, switch to a playback mode.

TROUBLESHOOT PROBLEMS

Error messages on a digital camera can interrupt your first photo session. However, you can solve the most common problems quickly and easily.

The Shutter Release Button Does Not Work

If the shutter release button does not work, then the memory card may be locked. Take out the memory card and switch the lever or tab to the unlocked position. When the card is full, you can move the lever to the Lock position to protect images from accidental deletion. For more about memory cards, see Chapter 2.

The Camera Is On, But You Cannot Take Pictures

To conserve battery power, most cameras go into sleep mode when they are not in use for a while. You can press the main power button to wake up the camera, or you can turn the camera off and then turn it back on. Also, check to see if the memory card is full, or if the battery needs to be recharged or replaced.

When You Cannot Save Images

When the memory card is full, your camera displays a message that images cannot be saved. To save new images, you can either insert an empty memory card or delete pictures from the card in the camera.

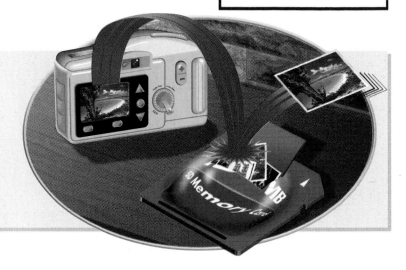

© 2004 Charlotte K. Lowrie

Flash Pictures Are Too Dark

All built-in flash units work within a range specified by the manufacturer, usually up to 15 feet. If flash pictures in the LCD look too dark, the subject may be too far away. Move closer to the subject, and check the camera manual for the flash distance range.

Pictures Are Blurry

Digital cameras include a focus indicator on the back of the camera. Always check that the focus indicator shows good focus before taking the picture. Check the scene mode settings; pictures can be blurry if you take a landscape shot with the camera set to macro mode. Also see if the lens needs cleaning.

DOWNLOAD PICTURES TO THE COMPUTER

When the memory card is full of pictures, you can transfer them to the computer for evaluation. Learn the options for transferring and viewing your images.

Why Transfer Pictures to the Computer?

By reviewing pictures on the computer, you can decide whether the camera settings need adjustment. You can use the software that came with the camera on your computer to view the pictures, or an image-editing program, such as Adobe Photoshop Elements.

What about RAW-format Images?

If you take RAW-format pictures, then use the manufacturer's software to view and edit the images. In most RAW conversion programs, you can correct or fine-tune exposure settings including aperture and white balance. After you save the images in TIFF OR JPEG format, you can open and continue editing images in programs such as Adobe Photoshop Elements or Microsoft Digital Image Pro.

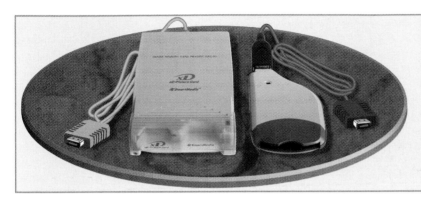

Transfer Options

How you download images depends on your camera. Your camera may have a dock that plugs into the computer. You can also use a USB cable, a separately purchased memory-card reader, or a PC adapter card. Each camera interacts with the computer differently. Consult your camera manual for information about your particular camera.

The Easiest Transfer Technique

To download pictures, you can use the supplied USB cord to plug into the computer and the camera. Ensure that the camera battery is fully charged. With a laptop computer, you can insert the memory card into a PC card adapter, and then insert the adapter into your laptop. For dockable cameras, insert the camera into the dock, and press the Upload button. Most computer operating systems display a connected digital camera as a separate disk drive.

Disconnect the Camera and Clear the Card

To disconnect the camera from your computer, first ensure that the access indicator light is off, and then click the Windows task bar Unplug or Eject Hardware icon. Then unplug the USB cable.

To clear the card, turn the camera on. You can delete the pictures from the memory card by choosing the Format Card option on one of the camera menus.

EVALUATE PICTURES

You cannot tell how good your test pictures are until you see them on the computer. This is your chance to identify camera settings you may want to change.

Identify Recurring Issues

Evaluating your first images allows you to determine any recurring correction issues. For example, if all or many of the images seem slightly too red or too yellow, or if images are slightly overexposed or underexposed, then you can use camera compensation options or your image-editing program to correct the pictures.

Evaluate Exposure

Different cameras can exhibit different exposure characteristics. If all the pictures look consistently too dark, then the camera may underexpose the images, provided that you used the correct settings when you took the picture. If the pictures consistently look too light, then the camera may overexpose images, or the flash intensity is too strong.

Evaluate Color

Most cameras tend toward certain color characteristics. Providing you set the white balance correctly, look for unnatural color casts, including a tendency toward a warm, red cast, or yellow or green cast. If you find a color cast, many cameras enable you to fine-tune color and white balance settings for indoor light settings, described later in the section "Fine-Tune Camera Settings."

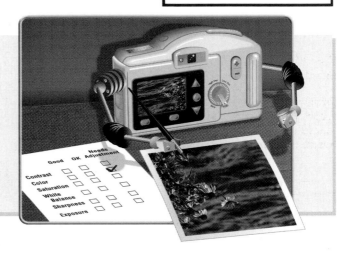

Evaluate Saturation and Contrast

Go through the pictures and evaluate the saturation, which is the intensity of color, and the contrast, which is the difference between light and dark tones. For your baseline set of pictures, evaluate whether the colors are too intense or unnaturally vibrant. Be sure that your computer monitor is calibrated correctly and often, as described in Chapter 10.

Do Not Worry about Sharpness

When you look at digital pictures on a computer monitor, they may seem *soft*, not as crisp as film prints. Although you can set higher sharpening settings on most cameras, resist the urge. You can sharpen images as the last step in editing. You sharpen images based on the final image size and whether you want to print or use the picture on the Web.

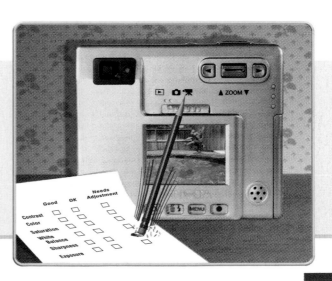

FINE-TUNE CAMERA SETTINGS

Fine-tuning camera settings saves you time and helps prevent recurring image characteristics that can be difficult to correct on the computer.

Make a List of Settings to Fine-Tune

Your first foray into using the digital camera provides an overview of the camera's capabilities in normal shooting situations, using the default settings. Now you know which settings to adjust and which ones to leave as they are. Make a list of the settings you want to adjust, and then begin by making small adjustments. Then evaluate the results.

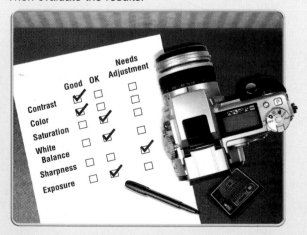

Why Fine-Tune the Camera Settings?

You want to begin image editing with the best quality image you can get from the camera. This saves you time, and makes image editing much more enjoyable. Although image-editing software is powerful, it cannot fix some things, including poor focus, heavy-color casts, and overexposed images.

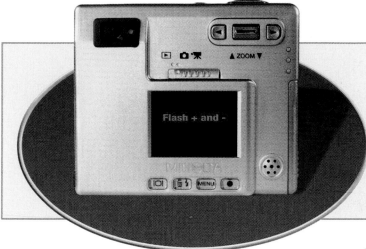

Fine-tune the Flash

If flash pictures are overexposed or too light, you can adjust the flash intensity by choosing a minus setting on the camera flash menu. If you do not have a flash adjustment option, you can set a minus exposure value (Ev) when you take a flash picture. You can experiment to see which setting produces a good exposure.

Fine-tune the Exposure

Scenes with large expanses of very dark or very light areas can fool the camera meter so that pictures are overexposed and underexposed, respectively. You can set exposure compensation, or a plus or minus exposure value (Ev), to get a picture with normal tonal values.

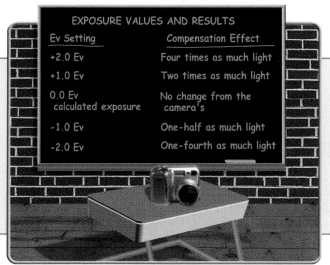

EXPOSURE VALUES AND RESULTS	
Ev Setting	Compensation Effect
+2.0 Ev	Four times as much light
+1.0 Ev	Two times as much light
0.0 Ev calculated exposure	No change from the camera's
-1.0 Ev	One-half as much light
-2.0 Ev	One-fourth as much light

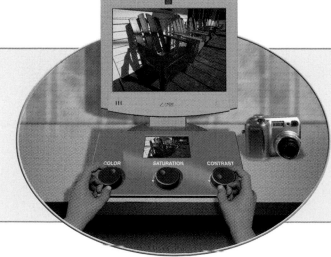

Fine-Tune Color, Saturation, and Contrast

Newer digital cameras offer options to increase color, saturation, and contrast. Never adjust settings based on LCD images which is too small to accurately show these characteristics. Instead, evaluate a large sampling of representative pictures on the computer and as prints. If the color, saturation, or contrast is consistently off, then adjust in small increments until you get the pictures you want.

CHAPTER 9

Avoid Digital Photography Pitfalls

In this chapter, you learn how to recognize and avoid the most common problems in digital photography.

AVOID TAKING UNFIXABLE PICTURES

Just as with a film camera, you can take digital pictures that have problems that no amount of computer image editing can fix. You can learn the most common digital photography problems and how to avoid them.

What Are Unfixable Photo Problems?

Unfixable digital photo problems include excessively overexposed pictures, pictures with excessive *digital noise* — unwanted multi-colored pixels throughout the image — and blurry pictures. Use the tips in this chapter to avoid taking unfixable pictures as well as other common digital photography problems.

WHAT IS A HISTOGRAM?

You can tell if an image is properly exposed by looking at the distribution of light, medium, and dark tones, shown on the image histogram on the camera or in an image-editing program.

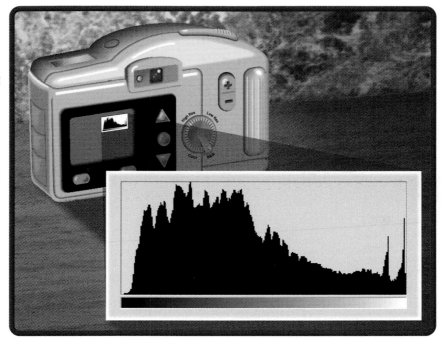

Not all digital cameras offer a histogram feature. Refer to your manual for details.

What a Histogram Shows

A histogram shows the distribution of tones, or the *contrast*, in an image. Brightness from black (on the left) to white, appears on the horizontal axis. The vertical axis shows the number, or weight, of pixels at each brightness level. In an average scene, a well-exposed image shows tonal distribution and weight distributed fairly evenly across the entire histogram.

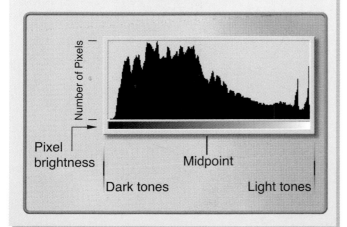

How to Identify Problem Pictures

In pictures of an average scene, if most of the pixels fall to the left of center, then the picture is *underexposed*, or too dark, as shown here. Conversely, if most of pixels fall to the right of center, then the picture is *overexposed*, or too light. A thin horizontal line shows that very little detail exists in that tonal range.

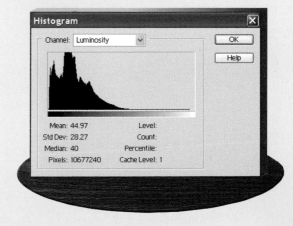

USE A HISTOGRAM AS YOU TAKE PICTURES

On most digital cameras, you can judge whether a picture is properly exposed, by looking at the histogram right after you take the picture.

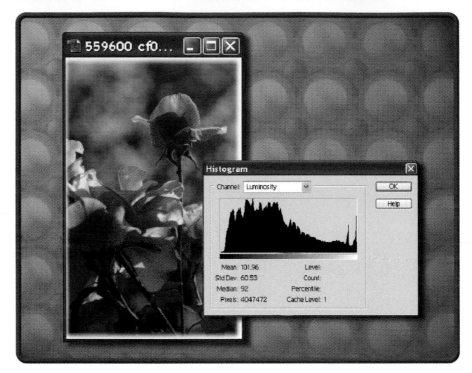

Turn on the Histogram Display

To see if your camera offers a histogram display, check the playback display options, or check the camera manual. Sometimes you may need to scroll through image information pages to get to the histogram in playback mode.

Use Overexposure Warning

If your camera offers a histogram display, you can use the *overexposure warning* — a small version of the picture — to see if areas of the image are too light. On the display, overexposed areas in the picture flash or are outlined. The display also shows exposure information and exposure compensation.

Does the Overexposure Warning Flash?

If the overexposure display flashes in certain areas, then note the exposure settings shown. You can then move the subject to a less bright area, or choose an exposure compensation setting, such as -1.0 Ev, that lets half as much light into the camera. Take the picture again and check the histogram.

Non-Average Scene Histograms

When scenes are predominately dark or light, the histogram reflects the predominate tones. For example, if you take a picture of a white wall, then the pixels fall on the right side of the histogram.

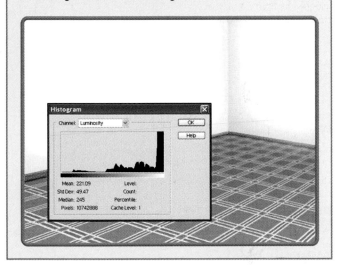

High-Key Histograms

In *high-key* scenes, with mostly light tones, most of the brightness pixels fall to the right of the histogram, even with an accurate exposure, as shown here. In high-key scenes, try to ensure that you do not have areas so bright that the camera records no detail in the picture.

Low-Key Histograms

In *low-key* scenes, with mostly dark tones, most of the brightness pixels fall to the left of the histogram, even with an accurate exposure, as shown here. In low-key scenes, try to ensure that darker shadow areas retain detail by ensuring that the scene is not overexposed You can also regain some shadow detail using the midtone adjustment in the Levels dialog box.

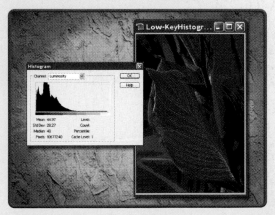

WORK AROUND SHUTTER LAG

Unlike film cameras that instantly take a picture when you press the shutter release button, many digital cameras delay before taking the picture. You can learn how to work around the delay to avoid missing the action.

What Is Shutter Lag?

The delay between the time you press the shutter release button and the time when the camera takes the picture is called *shutter lag*. Because of this delay, you can miss capturing the action, such as the moment a family member blows out candles on a birthday cake, or a top as it spins.

Avoid Missing Critical Moments

To work around shutter lag, you can anticipate the action. Focus on where the action will happen and press the shutter release button halfway down, wait for the action, and then take the picture. You should also turn off red-eye reduction if you use a flash, and you should remove accessory lenses and avoid using extreme zoom settings. Also switch to burst mode to capture a rapid sequence of pictures with no shutter lag.

You can fix many problems in image-editing programs, but you cannot fix areas of the image where the camera records no details. You can learn how to avoid blowing out the highlight details.

© 2004 Charlotte K. Lowrie

What Are Blown Highlights?

When you take pictures in a scene with very bright and very dark areas, the brightness differences may exceed the camera's *dynamic range*, or its ability to record both very bright and very dark areas. As a result, very bright areas often lack detail and appear as solid white.

© 2004 Charlotte K. Lowrie

How to Avoid Blown Highlights

It is particularly important to avoid highlight blowout, in the main subject area. To avoid blown highlights, switch to a semi-automatic or manual mode, and then select spot or center-weighted metering. The camera meter weighs exposure primarily for light falling on the subject rather than averaging the entire scene, ensuring accurate subject exposure, as shown here.

CENTER-WEIGHT
Center 80% Balance 20%

KEEP LIGHTWEIGHT CAMERAS STEADY

Small, lightweight cameras invite a lot of everyday, impromptu snapshots. But the camera's light weight can also mean blurry pictures. You can learn how to get sharp pictures with small cameras.

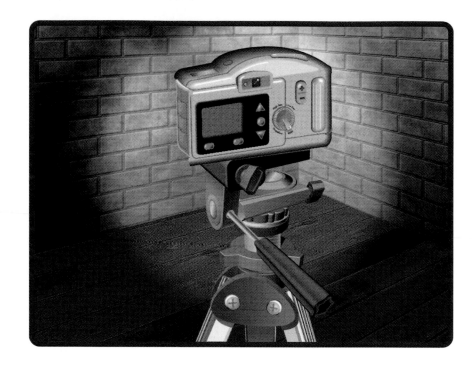

What Is Camera Shake?

Newer pocket- and palm-size digital cameras make everyday snaps inviting and easy. Because of their low weight, avoiding *camera shake* — blur from hand movement during shooting — can be challenging. Some cameras include a camera shake warning that indicates when you should steady the camera, especially in low-light scenes. Be sure to turn on the indicator if you have a small camera.

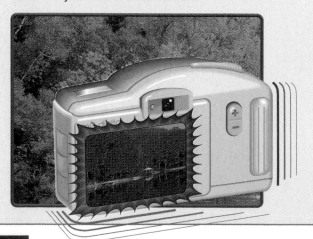

How to Avoid Camera Shake

In all but very bright scenes, you need to steady the camera by leaning against a solid surface like a wall, or by setting the camera on a solid surface when taking the picture. Alternately, you can buy a tabletop tripod that ensures sharp images.

AVOID INACCURATE COLOR CASTS

With digital cameras, you can easily avoid taking pictures that have an unwanted color cast. Setting the camera to get accurate color also saves time when you edit images on the computer.

·LIGHTING·
- ○ OUTDOOR
- ○ INDOOR
- ○ FLASH

What Causes Inaccurate Color Casts?

In all but very bright scenes, you need to steady the camera by leaning against a solid surface like a wall, or by setting the camera on a solid surface when taking the picture. Alternately, you can buy a tabletop tripod that ensures sharp images.

Set White Balance to Get Accurate Color

On digital cameras, you can set the white balance to the appropriate type of light for the scene and avoid taking pictures with unnatural color casts. To set the white balance, use the camera's menu — usually the shooting menu — to select a setting that matches the scene light, such as daylight, fluorescent, or tungsten (common household light).

107

DO NOT USE DIGITAL ZOOM

Although some cameras advertise extreme zoom capability, digital zoom produces a lower-quality picture than optical zoom.

How Digital Zoom Works

With digital zoom, the camera takes the center of the image, crops the edges, and then expands the center section to full-image size. Some cameras *interpolate*, or add pixels into the image, to bring the image to full resolution size. Because interpolation guesses where to add pixels to the image, the results are never as good as using optical zoom.

How to Avoid Using Digital Zoom

On some digital cameras, you can turn off digital zoom by selecting an option on one of the camera's menus. Most cameras with digital zoom include an audible signal or LCD indicator to tell you when to move from optical to digital zoom. Use the indicators to avoid activating the digital zoom feature.

REDUCE DIGITAL NOISE

Multicolor flecks or pixels in dark areas of a low-light picture ruin digital images. You can avoid getting digital noise by following these simple guidelines.

Recognize Digital Noise

With digital zoom, the camera takes the center of the image, crops the edges, and then expands the center section to full-image size. Some cameras *interpolate*, or add pixels into the image, to bring the image to full resolution size. Because interpolation guesses where to add pixels to the image, the results are never as good as using optical zoom.

How to Avoid Digital Noise

Both high ISO settings and long exposures contribute to digital noise. To prevent digital noise, select lower ISO settings, such as ISO 200 or lower, and then use a tripod or steady shooting surface. You can also select a scene mode appropriate for low-light scenes, or use the flash to avoid long exposures.

AVOID IN-CAMERA ADJUSTMENTS

Newer digital cameras offer options to increase or decrease picture contrast and saturation in the camera. Learn to use these adjustments cautiously, and only after evaluating test pictures to avoid an unnatural look.

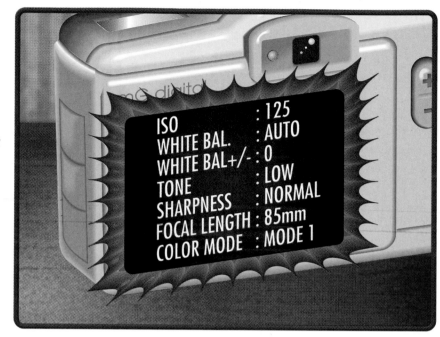

ISO	: 125
WHITE BAL.	: AUTO
WHITE BAL+/-	: 0
TONE	: LOW
SHARPNESS	: NORMAL
FOCAL LENGTH	: 85mm
COLOR MODE	: MODE 1

Avoid High-Contrast Settings

More and more cameras offer options for adjusting image sharpness, contrast, and color saturation. While these can be useful for snapshots, they also produce images that look artificially enhanced. If your camera offers a contrast level adjustment, then you should not select the high-contrast option to avoid taking contrasted images.

Avoid Increased Saturation Settings

Options for increasing *saturation*, or intensity of colors, add vibrancy to the colors but they also produce images that look unnaturally vivid. If you want more vivid images, then wait to increase saturation in an image-editing program.

LEARN YOUR CAMERA'S CHARACTERISTICS

Camera characteristics vary by type and manufacturer. Learning your camera's characteristics and adjusting for them can produce consistently better pictures.

Fine-Tune Exposure Settings

After several weeks of taking pictures with your camera, you can tell if the camera consistently overexposes or underexposes images. You can select positive or negative exposure value (Ev) settings to compensate for consistent exposure problems. For example, if the camera overexposes images (they are too light) then choose a minus Ev setting.

Fine-Tune White Balance and Flash Settings

Like exposure settings, you can adjust settings, such as white balance and flash intensity, on many digital cameras. For example, if you take pictures indoors under the same kind of household light, then you can select a positive or negative tungsten white balance setting to get more accurate color. You can also adjust the flash to reduce the output for better flash picture results, as shown here.

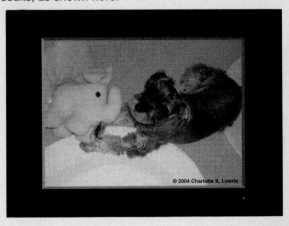

© 2004 Charlotte K. Lowrie

CHAPTER 10

Retouch Images in Photoshop Elements

You can crop and fine-tune color, contrast, and the saturation of your digital images. This chapter introduces the basics of digital image editing.

LEARN ABOUT IMAGE-EDITING PROGRAMS

With digital images, you can correct many photo problems, including color, contrast, and red eye.

Image-Editing Programs

You can choose from a variety of image-editing programs. In fact, many digital cameras include an image-editing program. Some programs, such as Adobe Photoshop Elements, allow you to view and organize digital images.

What You Can Do in Image-Editing Programs

With image-editing programs, you can correct color, contrast, saturation, red eye, and remove or add elements, such as people, objects, and text, to a picture. You can also resize pictures to send to friends and family in e-mail messages. You can print a picture on your home photo printer, or send it for printing to a commercial photo lab.

THE IMAGE-EDITING PROCESS

The image-editing process consists of a sequence of adjustments. It is a good idea to do the steps in the sequence because each step builds on the previous step.

Why Follow a Process?

Following a sequence, or *workflow,* in the digital darkroom not only helps you to obtain the best results, but also ensures that you work with a high-resolution copy of the image for as long as you can before making final edits, such as cropping or resizing for printing.

The Editing Process

The basic image-editing workflow includes these corrections and steps:

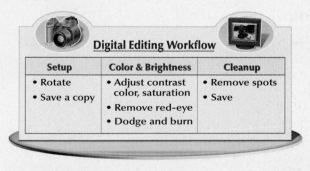

Digital Editing Workflow

Setup	Color & Brightness	Cleanup
• Rotate • Save a copy	• Adjust contrast color, saturation • Remove red-eye • Dodge and burn	• Remove spots • Save

CALIBRATE YOUR MONITOR

You can calibrate your computer monitor to remove any color cast the monitor has. Adobe Photoshop Elements provides an easy-to-use calibration utility for creating and saving a calibrated monitor profile.

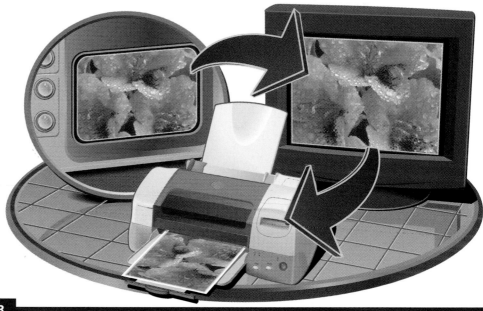

CALIBRATE YOUR MONITOR

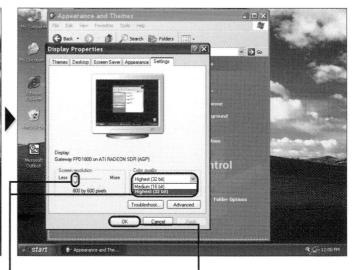

SET UP YOUR MONITOR

1 Click **Start**.

2 Click **Control Panel**.

■ The Windows Control Panel appears.

3 Click **Appearance and Themes**.

■ The Appearance and Themes dialog box appears.

4 Click **Change the screen resolution**.

■ The Display Properties dialog box appears.

5 Click ✓ to change the Color quality to **Medium (16 bit)** or higher.

■ Dragging 🗍 to the right increases the screen resolution, which enables you to easily work with the Photoshop Elements Palette Well.

6 Click **OK**.

■ Windows applies the new color quality.

Why calibrate a monitor?

Calibrating your monitor is the first step in ensuring that what you see on the monitor matches the prints that you make on your home photo printer.

Should I buy a special calibration device?

Some calibration devices precisely measure the color of your monitor. Other devices calibrate the monitor and the printer, and create profiles to ensure an exact match between the monitor and the printed photos. Unless you get dramatically different color between the monitor and the printed photo, the Adobe calibration program provides adequate results.

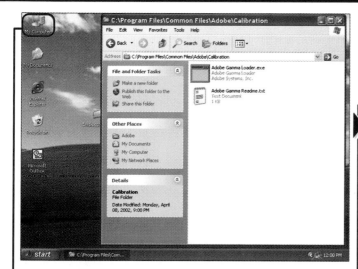

**START THE ADOBE GAMMA
CALIBRATION PROGRAM**

1 Double-click **My Computer.**

2 Double-click **Local Disk (C:).**

■ Windows displays a list of folders and files on your computer hard drive.

3 Double-click **Program Files.**

4 Double-click **Common Files.**

5 Double-click **Adobe.**

6 Double-click **Calibration.**

7 Double-click **Adobe Gamma.cpl.**

CONTINUED

CALIBRATE YOUR MONITOR

Calibrating a monitor
helps ensure that colors
appear true when other
people with calibrated
monitors view your
pictures.

Calibrated / **Uncalibrated**

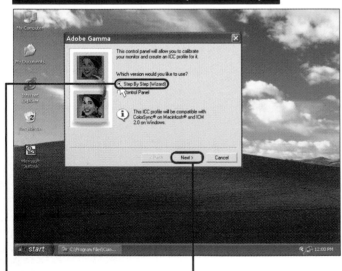

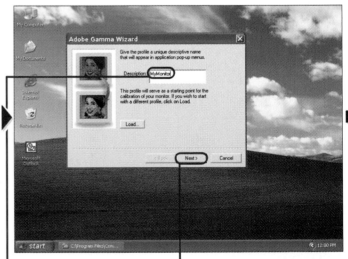

■ The Adobe Gamma dialog
box appears.

9 Click **Next.**

8 Click **Step By Step**
(○ changes to ◉).

10 Type a name for
the profile.

11 Click **Next.**

*Note: This example uses the profile
name MyMonitorProfile.*

118

Is there anything I should do before I calibrate my monitor?

For the best calibration results, turn on your monitor 30 minutes before you calibrate it. Also, before you start the Adobe Gamma wizard, darken the room.

What difference does the white point of the monitor make?

The white point affects how colors display on your screen. As a comparison, the white point of a blank piece of white paper is 5000 Kelvin (K), while the default Windows white point is 6500K. When you choose a lower value, colors look warmer on the screen, while choosing a higher value makes colors appear cooler or whiter.

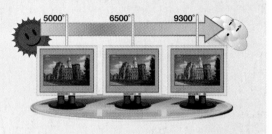

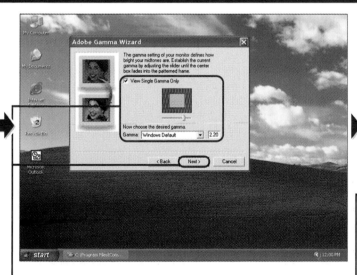

12 Complete each step in the wizard and click Next to continue.

13 Click **Finish** when you are done.

14 Type a name for the monitor profile.

15 Click **Save.**

START ADOBE PHOTOSHOP ELEMENTS

The first step in editing digital images is to start Adobe Photoshop Elements and to become familiar with the program. You can access the tutorial from the opening screen for a guided tour.

START ADOBE PHOTOSHOP ELEMENTS

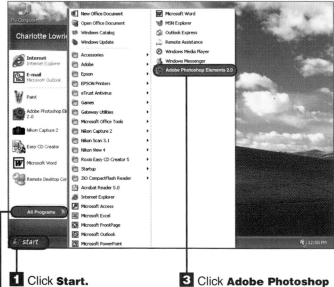

1 Click **Start**.

2 Click **All Programs**.

3 Click **Adobe Photoshop Elements 2.0**.

■ Photoshop Elements starts.

■ A window appears with shortcuts to the most common Photoshop Elements tasks.

■ You can click **Exit Welcome Screen** to close the window.

■ You can click **Show this screen at startup** (☐ changes to ☑) to avoid the window in the future.

THE PHOTOSHOP ELEMENTS WORKSPACE

You can use tools and
menu commands to open
and edit digital images.

Shortcuts Bar

Contains icons you
can click to perform
actions and to
access Help.

Options Bar

Contains controls
that allow you to
customize the tool
you select from
the toolbox.

Elements Toolbox

Contains image-
editing tools to
correct your picture.
To use most tools,
you click the tool
and drag it inside
the picture to make
corrections.

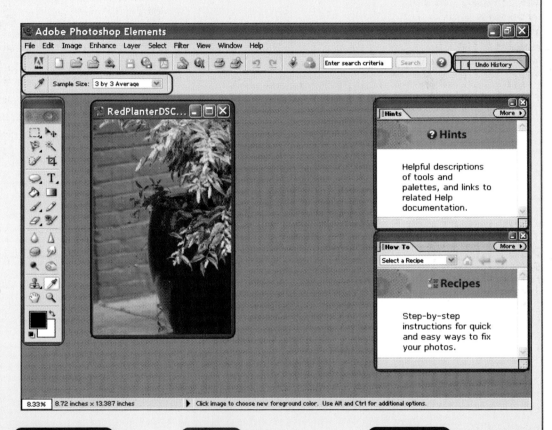

Image Window

Displays the image in
which you are working.

Palettes

Floating windows that
provide access to tools,
options, and commands.

Palette Well

Palettes you can use to add
effects, access Help, and
undo editing changes. You
can drag palettes from the
Palette Well to the workspace
to keep them open.

GET HELP

As you work, you can get answers to your questions and learn more about Photoshop Elements, by using the Help system.

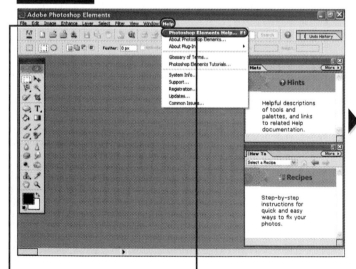

1 Click **Help**.

2 Click **Photoshop Elements Help**.

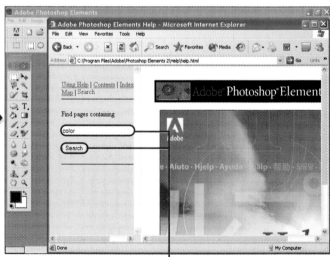

■ Photoshop Elements displays Help topics in a Web browser window.

3 Type a word describing the task with which you want help.

4 Click **Search**.

What are recipes?

Recipes tell you how to do common tasks, such as correcting color, and take you to commands for doing some of the steps or perform them for you.

■ Photoshop Elements displays step-by-step instructions for completing the task.

1 Click ✔.

2 Click the recipe you want.

3 In the list of topics, click the topic you want.

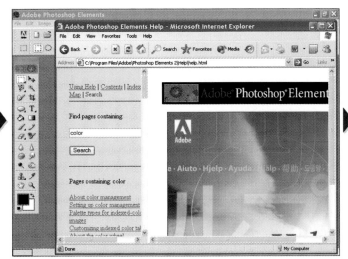

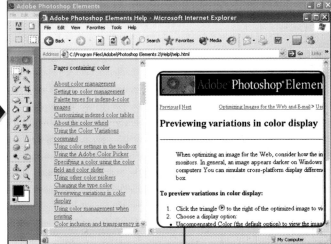

■ Photoshop Elements displays a list of topics.

5 Click the topic you want.

■ Photoshop Elements displays the Help topic.

For access to additional Photoshop Elements tools, you can open free-floating windows called *palettes* from the Palette Well.

OPEN PALETTES

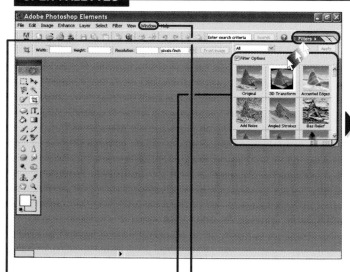

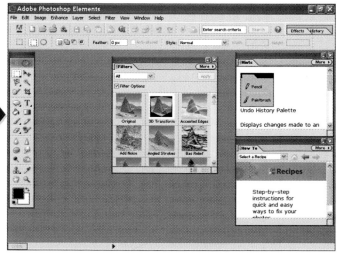

1 Click a tab in the Palette Well.

■ The palette opens.

■ You can also click **Window,** and then click the name of the palette you want to open.

2 Click and drag the palette to the work area.

■ When you release the mouse button, the palette remains open in the work area.

How do I enlarge the Palette Well?

If you find that the Palette Well is too small to use comfortably, then you can change the resolution of your monitor, which increases the size of the Palette Well.

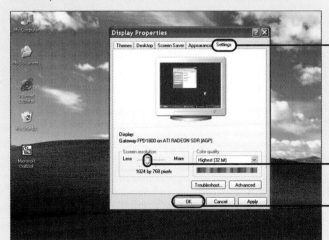

1 Right-click the Windows desktop and select **Properties** from the menu.

■ The Display Properties dialog box appears.

2 Click the **Settings** tab.

3 Click and drag 🖑 to the right to decrease the resolution.

4 Click **OK**.

■ The screen resolution changes.

CLOSE PALETTES

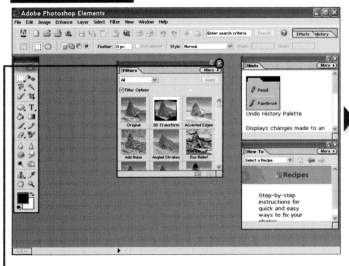

1 Click ✕.

■ You can also click **Window**, and then click the palette name to close the palette.

■ Photoshop Elements closes the palette and stores it in the Palette Well.

OPEN A PICTURE

After you download your pictures to the computer, you can open one or more pictures in Photoshop Elements, and begin editing them.

OPEN A PICTURE

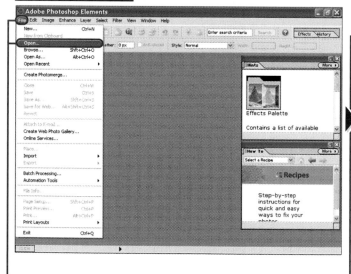

1 Click **File.**

2 Click **Open.**

■ You can also click 🖼.

■ The **Open** dialog box appears.

3 Click ⌄ to display additional folders.

4 Click the file of the picture you want to open.

What types of files can Photoshop Elements open?

Photoshop Elements can open most of the common image file formats in use today, including:

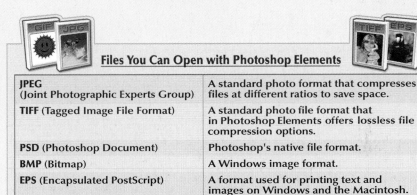

Files You Can Open with Photoshop Elements

JPEG (Joint Photographic Experts Group)	A standard photo format that compresses files at different ratios to save space.
TIFF (Tagged Image File Format)	A standard photo file format that in Photoshop Elements offers lossless file compression options.
PSD (Photoshop Document)	Photoshop's native file format.
BMP (Bitmap)	A Windows image format.
EPS (Encapsulated PostScript)	A format used for printing text and images on Windows and the Macintosh.
GIF (Graphics Interchange Format)	A format for Web images.

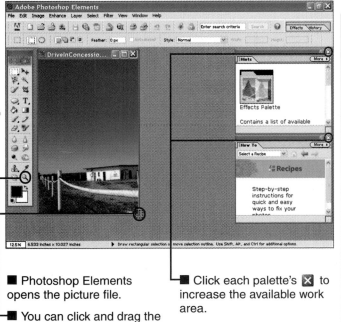

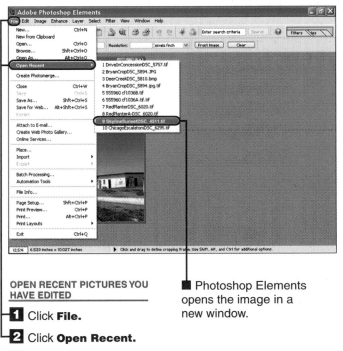

■ Photoshop Elements opens the picture file.

■ You can click and drag the edge of the picture to increase the window size, and then click the Zoom tool ( ) to enlarge the picture.

■ Click each palette's ☒ to increase the available work area.

OPEN RECENT PICTURES YOU HAVE EDITED

1 Click **File**.

2 Click **Open Recent**.

3 Click a file from the list.

■ Photoshop Elements opens the image in a new window.

BROWSE FOR A PICTURE

You can look for an image you worked on, as well as all images on your computer, by using the Photoshop Elements File Browser.

BROWSE FOR A PICTURE

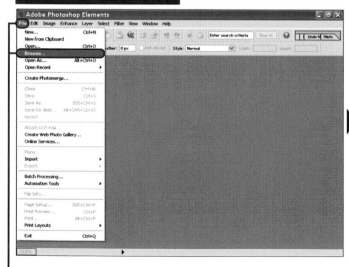

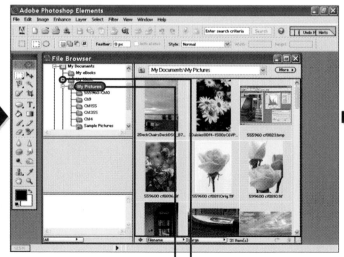

1 Click **File**.

2 Click **Browse**.

■ You can also click **Window** and then click **File Browser**.

■ Photoshop Elements displays the File Browser.

3 In the left pane, click ⊞ to display the subfolders.

4 Click a subfolder.

Where should I store images on my computer?

It is a good idea to store images in the My Pictures subfolder of the My Documents folder. Windows and other programs use the My Pictures folder as the default folder for image files. You can create subfolders within the My Pictures folder to organize your pictures in categories, such as family, events, and birthdays.

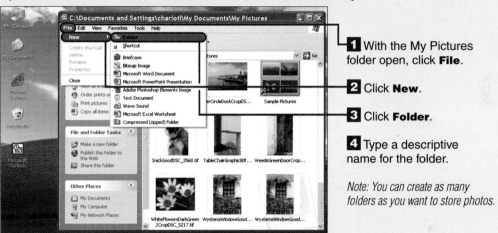

1 With the My Pictures folder open, click **File**.

2 Click **New**.

3 Click **Folder**.

4 Type a descriptive name for the folder.

Note: You can create as many folders as you want to store photos.

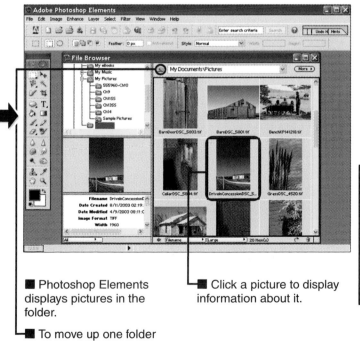

■ Photoshop Elements displays pictures in the folder.

■ To move up one folder level, click 🔼 .

■ Click a picture to display information about it.

OPEN A PICTURE

1 Double-click a thumbnail image.

■ Photoshop Elements opens the picture file.

INCREASE AND DECREASE IMAGE MAGNIFICATION

When you open an image in Photoshop Elements, Elements displays a reduced view of the image. You can enlarge the image on the screen to more easily edit it.

INCREASE AND DECREASE IMAGE MAGNIFICATION

INCREASE IMAGE MAGNIFICATION

1 Click the Zoom tool (🔍).

2 Click the image.

■ Photoshop Elements enlarges the image.

■ You can drag the edge of the window to view more of the picture.

■ The title bar and status bar display the percentage of magnification.

How do I display the image at 100% magnification?

With the , right-click within the image, and then click **Actual Pixels from the menu**. Viewing an image at 100% magnification most accurately displays image colors.

Actual Pixels

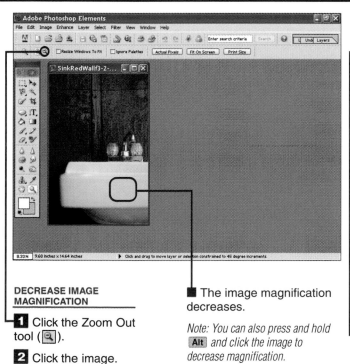

DECREASE IMAGE MAGNIFICATION

1 Click the Zoom Out tool (🔍).

2 Click the image.

■ The image magnification decreases.

Note: You can also press and hold Alt *and click the image to decrease magnification.*

MAGNIFY A DETAIL

1 Click the 🔍 tool.

2 Click and drag the Zoom In tool over the detail you want to magnify.

3 Release the mouse button.

■ Photoshop Elements magnifies the detail.

ROTATE AN IMAGE

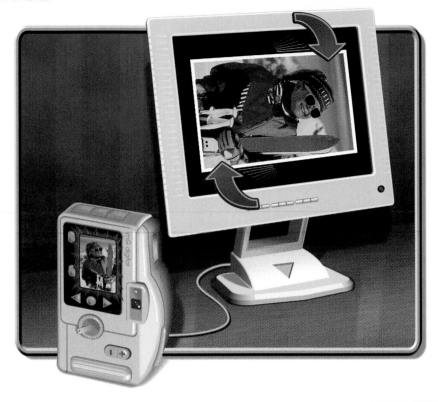

If you took a picture in a vertical orientation, then you can quickly rotate the picture in Photoshop Elements.

ROTATE AN IMAGE

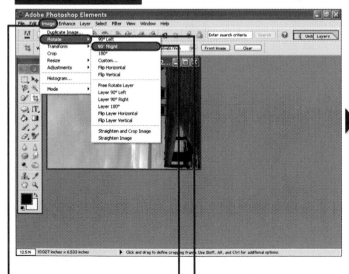

1 Click **Image.**

Note: See the section "Open a Picture" for instructions on opening pictures.

2 Click **Rotate.**

3 Click either **90° Left** or **90° Right**.

■ Photoshop Elements rotates the image.

UNDO CHANGES

Photoshop Elements
enables you to undo
many changes, either
one at a time or many
steps at a time. Just
back up using the Undo
History palette that
displays each of your
changes.

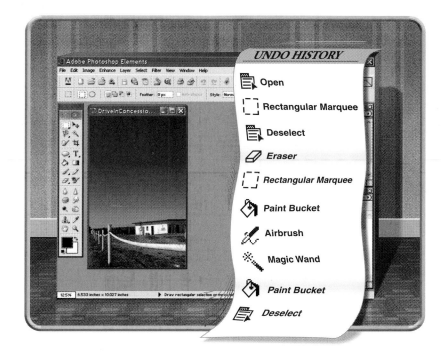

UNDO CHANGES

1 In the Palette Well, click
the **Undo History** tab.

2 Click and drag ⬇ up one
or more steps.

■ Photoshop Elements
undoes the changes.

■ You can also click the
Step Backward button (⬅)
to undo the last edit.

SAVE AND OPEN A COPY OF THE PICTURE

Before you edit a picture, be sure to make a copy of the original, and edit the copy. This ensures that if you do not like the final edited picture, then you can start over with the original image.

SAVE A COPY

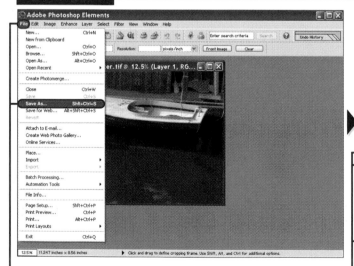

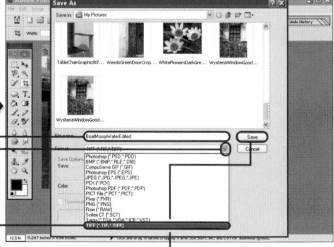

1 Click **File**.

2 Click **Save As**.

■ The Save As dialog box appears.

3 Type a name for the file.

4 Click ∨.

5 Select **TIFF** or **PSD**.

■ Use TIFF with LZW compression when saving images because this format and compression option retains all of the image data and images can be opened in most programs.

6 Click **Save**.

In which format should I save edited pictures?

Save your images in TIFF format with LZW compression or in PSD format. Neither format discards picture information by compressing the image. Choose TIFF if you want to share the picture with others, or open it on a computer that does not have Photoshop Elements installed.

What about pictures I use on the Web or send in e-mail?

For pictures that you use online, you want a small file size that downloads quickly from the Web, or that is small enough to send in e-mail. For these pictures, you can save a copy in JPEG format. JPEG format compresses the image, making the file size smaller.

OPEN A COPY OF THE IMAGE

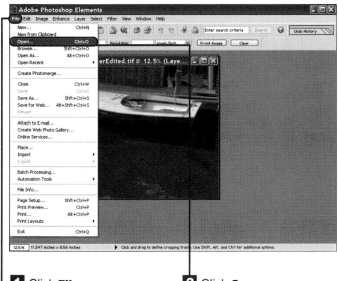

1 Click **File**.

2 Click **Open**.

■ The File Open dialog box appears.

3 Click the name of the image file you want to open.

4 Click **Open**.

■ Photoshop Elements opens the image.

SET WHITE AND BLACK POINT VALUES

You can set the White and Black Point values to help make automatic color and contrast adjustments more precise, and to remove color casts from pictures.

SET WHITE AND BLACK POINT VALUES

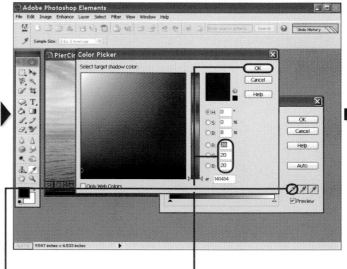

1 Open a picture.

2 Click **Enhance.**

3 Click **Adjust Brightness/Contrast.**

4 Click **Levels.**

■ The Levels dialog box appears.

SET THE SHADOW VALUE

5 Double-click the Set Black Point Eyedropper tool (✏).

■ The Color Picker dialog box appears.

6 Type **20** for the R, G, and B values.

7 Click **OK.**

■ In the Levels dialog box, click **OK.**

136

How do I set color preferences?

Color preferences determine the *color space*, or the number or range of colors, used. For best results, use the Photoshop Elements default color space selection, which is Adobe. To verify that Adobe is the default:

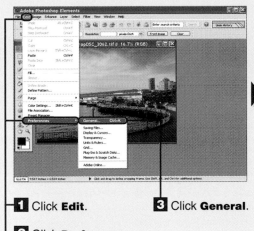

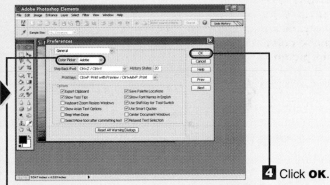

1 Click **Edit**.

2 Click **Preferences**.

3 Click **General**.

■ Verify that Adobe appears in the Color Picker box.

4 Click **OK**.

■ You can change additional Photoshop Elements preferences in the Preferences dialog box.

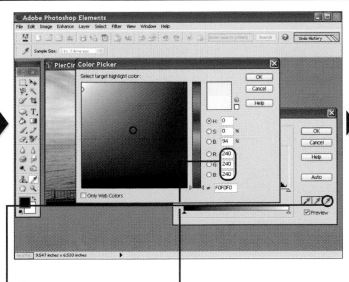

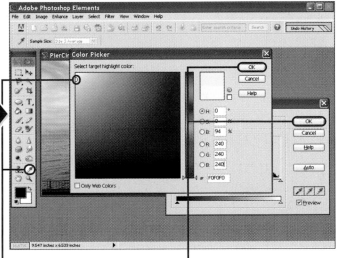

8 Double-click the Set White Point Eyedropper tool (■).

Note: When you select highlight and shadow colors, Photoshop Elements maps pixels to values that maintain good shadow and highlight detail for printing pictures.

■ The Color Picker dialog box appears.

9 Type **240** for the R, G, and B values.

10 Click ■ and then click an area of the picture that should be white.

11 Repeat step 10 using the Set Gray Point and Set Black Point Eyedropper tools, clicking gray and black points.

12 Click **OK**, then click **OK** again.

13 Click **Yes.**

ADJUST CONTRAST

When you adjust the contrast, Photoshop Elements redistributes the light-to-dark, or tonal, values in a picture. This section helps you ensure that pictures retain detail in the highlight and shadow areas.

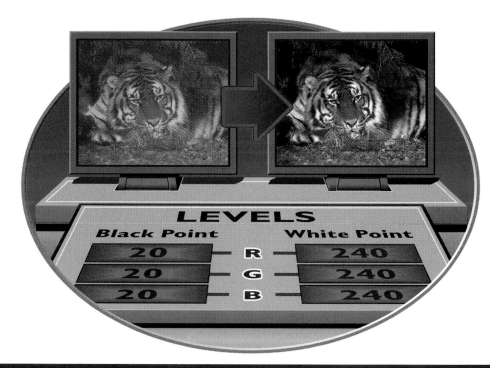

LEVELS

Black Point		White Point
20	R	240
20	G	240
20	B	240

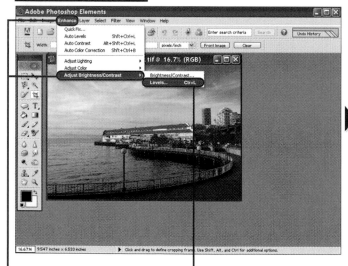

1 Click **Enhance.**

2 Click **Adjust Brightness/Contrast.**

3 Click **Levels.**

■ The Levels dialog box appears.

■ Verify that **Preview** is on (☐ changes to ☑).

4 Drag the first slider to the first large group of pixels.

5 Drag the second slider to the first large group of pixels.

6 Click **OK.**

■ If pixels in your picture are distributed evenly across the histogram, then skip step **4** or **5**, or both.

What tool should I use to adjust brightness?

The best tool you can use to adjust brightness is the **Midtone Input** slider in the **Levels** dialog box. This is because the method does not clip, or cut off pixels in the image.

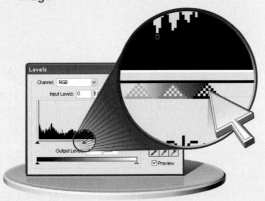

Setting the white and black points seems complicated. Do I have to do this for every picture?

After you set the white and black points described earlier, you can click **Auto** in the Levels dialog box, to make corrections automatically. If the adjustment looks good, then just adjust the midtones in the Levels dialog box. If you do not like the results, click **Undo** on the Edit menu.

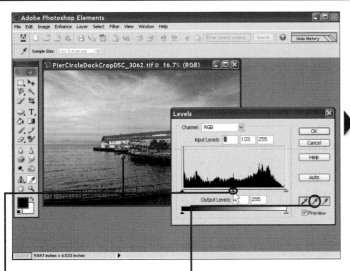

ADJUST MIDTONES

1 Drag the midtone slider to the left or right to adjust midtones.

■ Watch the image preview as you work, to ensure the corrections are acceptable.

■ You can click the Set Gray Point Eyedropper tool ( ), and then click a neutral gray area in the picture to adjust the midtones.

■ Photoshop Elements makes the tonal adjustments to the image.

ADJUST COLOR AND SATURATION

You can use color correction controls to correct color, hue, saturation, color casts, and make subtle improvements. For example, you can use the Color Variations command to adjust color brightness values in the highlight, midtone, and shadow areas of an image.

ADJUST COLOR

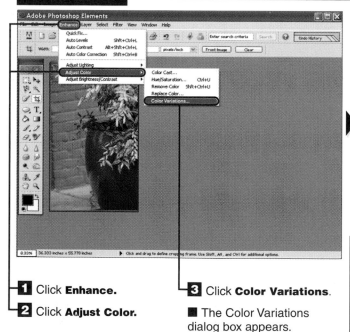

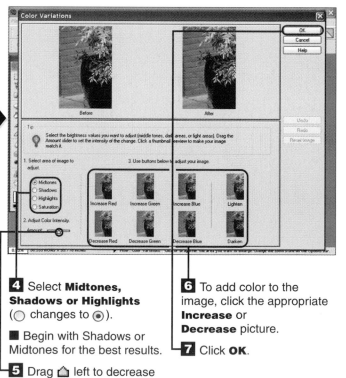

1 Click **Enhance**.

2 Click **Adjust Color**.

3 Click **Color Variations**.

■ The Color Variations dialog box appears.

4 Select **Midtones, Shadows or Highlights** (○ changes to ⦿).

■ Begin with Shadows or Midtones for the best results.

5 Drag △ left to decrease the amount of color or right to increase the amount.

6 To add color to the image, click the appropriate **Increase** or **Decrease** picture.

7 Click **OK**.

How do I balance colors?

To balance colors in a picture, you can subtract the color you do not want, or add the opposite color on the color wheel. For example, to decrease a magenta cast, you can remove red and blue, or you can add green, which is opposite magenta on the color wheel.

How do the Eyedropper tools work?

By default, the Eyedropper tools sample a single point, or pixel, in the picture. To get a more accurate sampling, especially if you want to correct skin tones in a picture, a 3-pixel by 3-pixel sampling size works best.

1 Click the **Eyedropper** tool (◢).

2 Click ⌄ and select **3 by 3 Average**.

ADJUST SATURATION

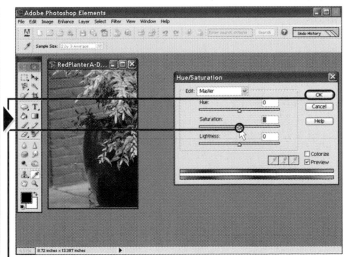

1 Click **Enhance**.

2 Click **Adjust Color**.

3 Click **Hue/Saturation**.

■ The Hue/Saturation dialog box appears.

4 Drag ⌂ to the left to decrease the vividness of the colors, or to the right to increase it.

5 Click **OK**.

■ Photoshop Elements makes the saturation changes to the image.

■ You can also correct color using the Auto Color Correction command on the Enhance menu.

CORRECT A COLOR CAST

While color balancing improves the colors in a picture, you can also adjust the overall colors in a picture quickly, with the Color Cast command.

CORRECT A COLOR CAST

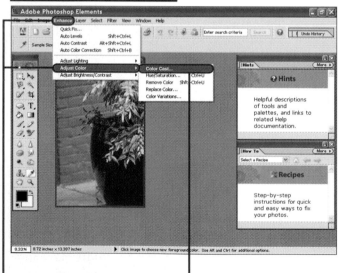

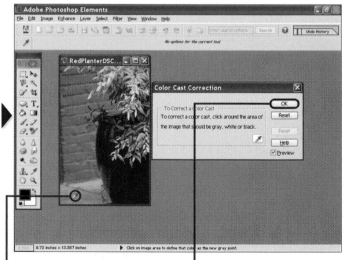

1 Click **Enhance**.

2 Click **Adjust Color**.

3 Click **Color Cast**.

■ The Color Cast Correction dialog box appears.

4 Click an area in the image that should be gray, white, or black.

■ Watch the picture to ensure that the color does not shift to a different color cast. If it does, click **Reset** to start over.

5 Click **OK**.

■ Photoshop Elements applies the correction to the picture.

By adding a slight blur
to areas of a picture,
you can remove dust
from digital camera
pictures, and dust and
scratches from pictures
you have scanned.

REMOVE DUST AND SCRATCHES

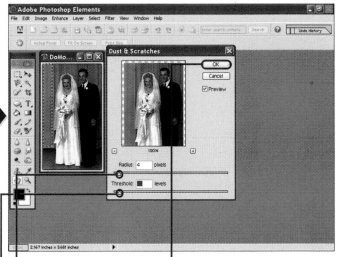

1 With a selection tool,
select an area in the picture
that contains dust
or scratches.

2 Click **Filter**.

3 Click **Noise**.

4 Click **Dust & Scratches**.

■ The Dust & Scratches
dialog box appears.

5 Drag ⌂ to set the size
for what Photoshop
Elements considers to be
dust or scratches.

6 Drag ⌂ to control how
many pixels differ from
surrounding pixels for
Photoshop Elements to
consider dust or scratches.

7 Click **OK**.

■ Photoshop Elements blurs
the dust and scratches in the
area you selected.

RETOUCH A PHOTO

You can remove small imperfections or make extensive changes to a photo using the Clone Stamp tool. The tool copies from one area of your photo into another to remove flaws or add elements.

RETOUCH A PHOTO

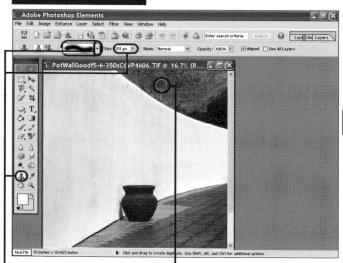

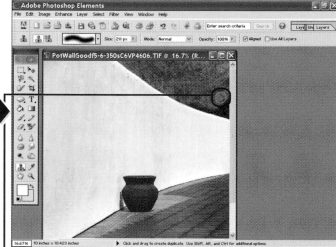

1 Click the Clone Stamp tool (⬛).

2 Click the Brush ▾.

3 Select the brush size and type you want.

■ The brush size and type changes.

4 While holding down Alt, click the area you want to copy.

5 Release the Alt key.

6 Click and drag the cursor in the area you want to change.

■ Elements copies from the area you selected to the area where you click and drag.

■ To clone large areas, resample often by repeating steps **1** and **2**.

144

Just as in a traditional
darkroom, you can
dodge, or lighten, and
burn, or darken,
selected areas of a
picture to improve its
appearance.

DODGE MIDTONES

BURN HIGHLIGHTS

DODGE AND BURN SELECTED AREAS

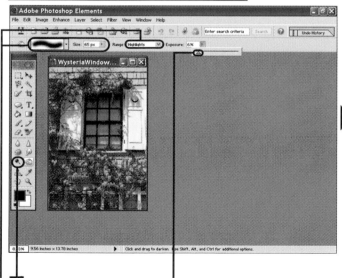

1 Click the Dodge tool
( ) to darken, or the Burn
tool ( ) to lighten areas.

2 Select the brush size and
type you want.

3 Select the range you
want.

■ To darken bright areas
with the Burn tool, select
Highlights. To lighten dark
areas with the Dodge tool,
select **Shadows**
or **Midtones**.

4 Click ▶ and then drag
⌂ to set the exposure.

5 Click and drag your
cursor over the areas you
want to darken or lighten.

■ You can change the
intensity of the effect by
increasing or decreasing the
opacity the areas you
dodged or burned.

REMOVE RED EYE

Red eye occurs when the camera flash reflects off the back of the eye. You can remove red eye with the Red Eye Brush tool.

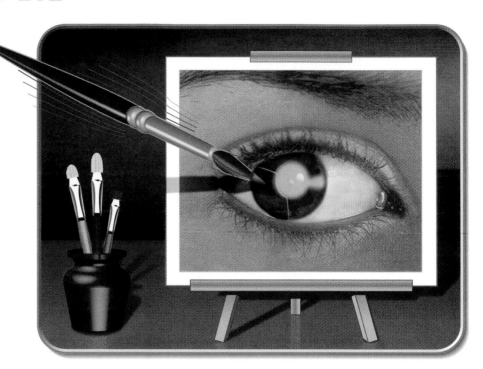

REMOVE RED EYE

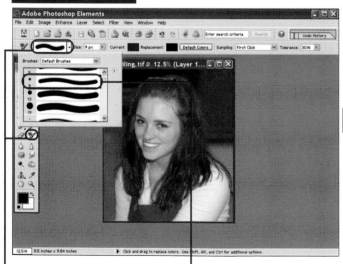

1 Click the Red Eye Brush tool (🖌️).

2 Select the brush type you want.

3 Select a size large enough to cover the subject's eye. Hold the brush over the eye to match the size.

■ Photoshop Elements displays the current color.

4 Click 🔲 to select a color other than default black.

■ Drag ◁ to move to different color hues.

Can I use the Red Eye Brush tool for other tasks?

You can use the Red Eye Brush tool to change other parts of a picture. For example, you can remove braces on teeth. Just choose a different color, in this case white, and paint over the braces.

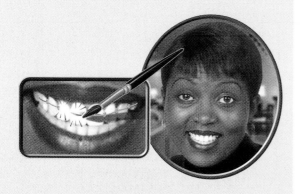

Why do cameras not remove red eye?

Presently, the best a camera can do is to fire a preflash that helps to close down the pupil and therefore, reduce the red that reflects from the back of the eye. You can also help reduce red eye by having the subject not look directly at the camera, as shown here.

5 Click ⌄ to change the tolerance.

■ The higher the number, the more red Photoshop Elements removes.

6 Click ⌄ and select **First Click**.

7 Drag △ to the left to decrease tolerance or to the right to increase it.

8 Click each red eye.

■ Photoshop Elements replaces the eye color with the replacement color.

ADJUST LIGHTING

In pictures where the light is behind the subject, the subject appears underexposed. You can add light to the subject using the Adjust Backlighting command. You can also lighten deep shadows caused by taking pictures in bright sunlight using the Fill Flash command.

ADJUST BACKLIT PICTURES

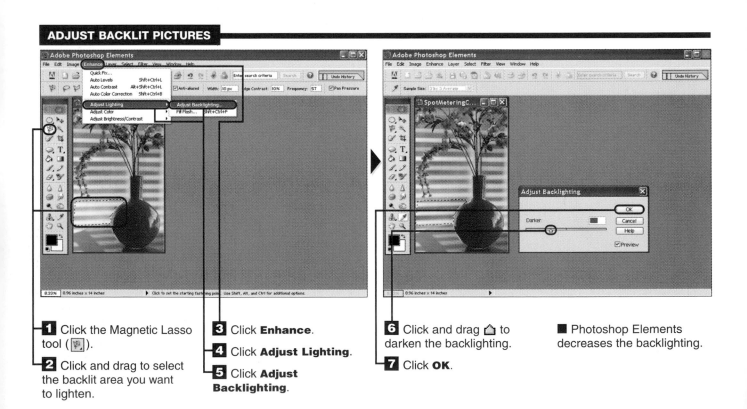

1 Click the Magnetic Lasso tool (🧲).

2 Click and drag to select the backlit area you want to lighten.

3 Click **Enhance**.

4 Click **Adjust Lighting**.

5 Click **Adjust Backlighting**.

6 Click and drag 🔺 to darken the backlighting.

7 Click **OK**.

■ Photoshop Elements decreases the backlighting.

Are there other ways to adjust for backlighting?

You can select the areas of the photo that are too dark, and then click **Enhance**, **Adjust Brightness/Contrast**, and then click **Levels**. Then click and drag the **Midtone** slider to increase the brightness.

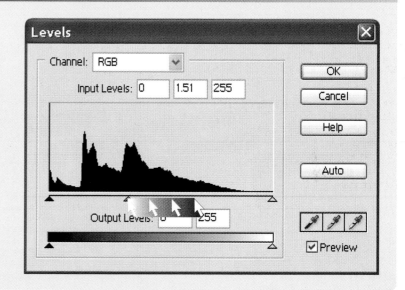

ADD FILL FLASH

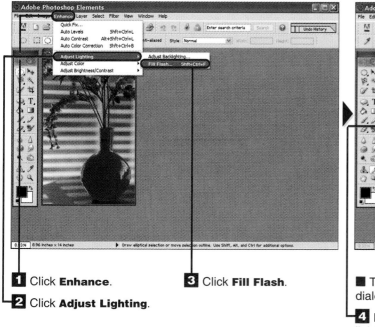

1 Click **Enhance**.

2 Click **Adjust Lighting**.

3 Click **Fill Flash**.

■ The Adjust Fill Flash dialog box appears.

4 Drag ⌂ to the right to lighten the image.

5 Drag ⌂ to the left to decrease the intensity, or saturation, of color, or to the right to increase it.

■ Increasing saturation helps counterbalance the increased image lightness from the fill flash.

CHAPTER 11

Create Effects

When editing digital images, you can straighten crooked photos, add text and frames, use artistic filters, and combine and stitch together multiple photos. This chapter shows you how.

STRAIGHTEN A CROOKED PHOTO

If you have pictures where the horizon seems to slide off to one side of the photo, then you can straighten the horizon line in Photoshop Elements.

STRAIGHTEN A CROOKED PHOTO

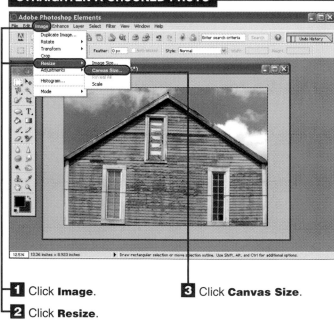

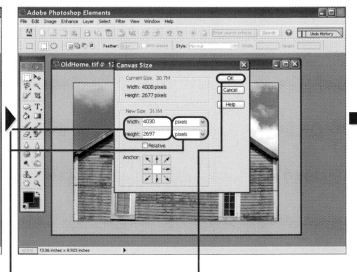

1 Click **Image**.

2 Click **Resize**.

3 Click **Canvas Size**.

■ The Canvas Size dialog box appears.

4 Click ⌄ and select the unit of measure.

5 Type a larger dimension in the Width and Height boxes.

6 Click **OK**.

■ Photoshop Elements resizes the canvas.

Is there another way to straighten a photo?

You can straighten a photo more using the Free Rotate command.

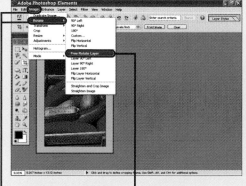

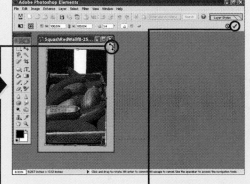

1 Click and drag the edge of the picture window to enlarge the window.

2 Click **Image**.

3 Click **Rotate**.

4 Click **Free Rotate Layer**.

■ If Elements asks if you want to make the picture a layer, click **OK**, type a name for the layer, and then click **OK**.

■ Elements selects the image.

5 In the area outside the picture, click and drag to rotate the picture.

6 Click ✓.

■ Alternately, you can press **Enter**

■ Elements straightens the image.

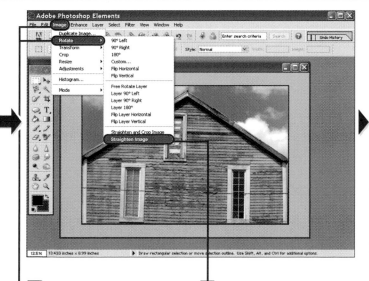

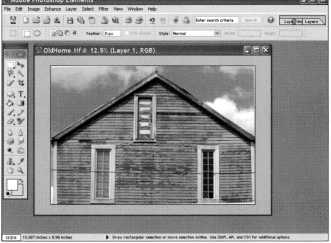

7 Click **Image**.

8 Click **Rotate**.

9 Click **Straighten Image**.

■ Photoshop Elements straightens the image.

■ You can simultaneously straighten and crop, but it is best to first check the results of rotating the image.

Note: For information on cropping a photo, see Chapter 12.

CORRECT WIDE-ANGLE DISTORTION

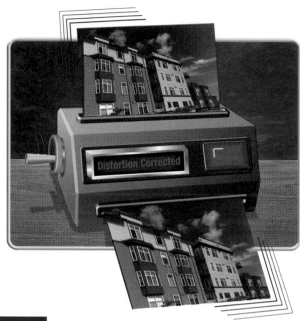

You can correct wide-angle distortion and keystoning or the apparent convergence of lines in a photo, by stretching elements in the picture back to straight angles or original proportions.

CORRECT WIDE-ANGLE DISTORTION

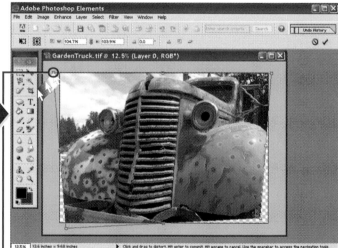

1 Click **Image**.

2 Click **Transform**.

3 Click **Skew**.

■ Click **OK** if Photoshop Elements asks if you want to make the picture the background layer, and then type a name for the layer.

■ Photoshop Elements selects the image, with selection handles along the edges.

4 Click and drag the picture window edge to enlarge the window.

5 Click and drag a handle to straighten lines.

6 Repeat step **4** for other corners of the picture.

■ Hold down Shift + Alt, and then click and drag to simultaneously move the top or bottom corners, or hold down Alt, and then click and drag to simultaneously move diagonal corners.

7 Press Enter.

■ Photoshop Elements straightens the image.

■ To crop the corrected image, click the Crop tool 🔲.

Note: See Chapter 12 to learn more about cropping photos.

154

CONVERT TO BLACK AND WHITE

Converting color images to black and white, or grayscale, creates photos reminiscent of the early days of photography. You can easily convert color to grayscale in Photoshop Elements.

CONVERT TO BLACK AND WHITE

−**1** Click **Enhance.**

−**2** Click **Adjust Color.**

3 Click **Hue/Saturation.**

■ The Hue and Saturation dialog box appears.

−**4** Drag △ to the far left to remove all color.

−**5** Click **OK.**

■ Photoshop Elements removes color from the image.

■ You can create a tinted image by moving the slider only part way to the left.

ADD FILM GRAIN

You can stylize a photo or make it look like an old photo by adding film grain.

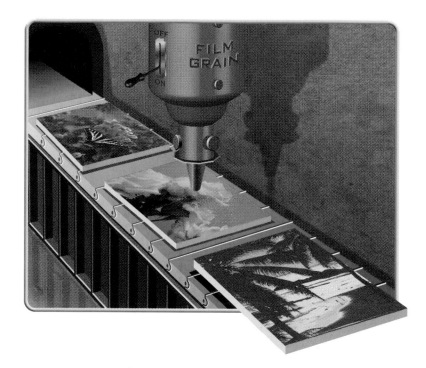

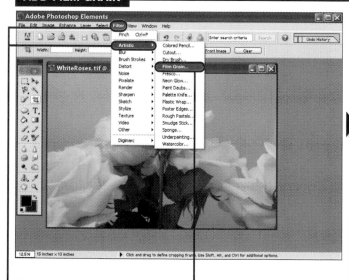

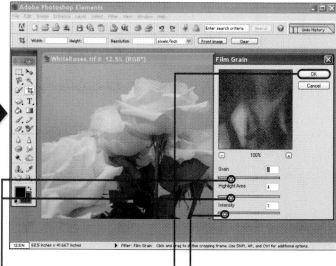

1 Click **Filter**.

2 Click **Artistic**.

3 Click **Film Grain**.

■ The Film Grain dialog box appears.

4 Drag ◻ left to decrease grain or right to increase it.

5 Drag ◻ left to decrease highlight area range or right to increase it.

6 Drag ◻ to select the intensity of the grain.

7 Click **OK**.

■ Photoshop Elements applies the grain to the picture.

CONVERT A PHOTO TO A SKETCH

With some photos, the Photoshop Elements Sketch filter can create a sketch-like version of a digital picture.

CONVERT A PHOTO TO A SKETCH

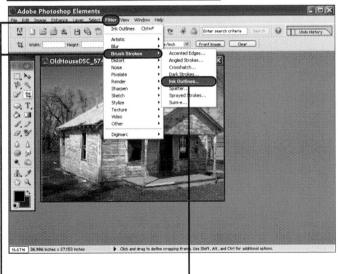

1 Click **Filter**.

2 Click **Brush Strokes**.

3 Click **Ink Outlines**.

■ The Ink Outlines dialog box appears.

4 Drag ⌂ left to decrease stroke length, or right to increase it.

5 Drag ⌂ to adjust the ratio of light to dark.

6 Click **OK**.

■ Photoshop Elements applies the filter.

■ You can adjust the color and brightness of the image.

ADD HORIZONTAL TEXT TO A PHOTO

You can add captions, labels, titles, and copyright lines to your photos by inserting horizontal text in the photos. You can also choose the style, font, and size of text.

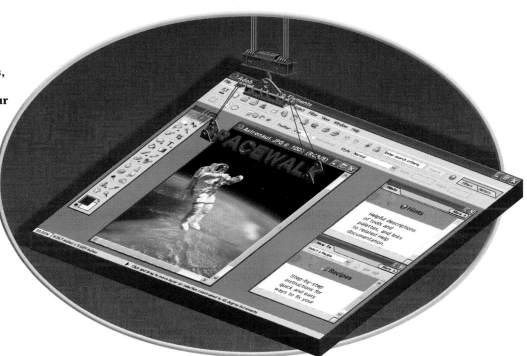

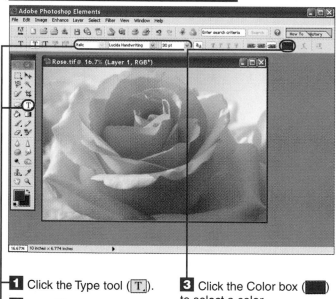

1 Click the Type tool (☐).

2 Click ☑ and select the style, font, and size for your text.

3 Click the Color box (▬) to select a color.

4 Click where you want the text to begin.

How do I move the text?

Since the text is on a layer, first display the Layers palette by clicking Window, and then clicking Layers. Then click the Move to)ol (). Click and drag the text to reposition it. You can move the text anywhere within the photo.

PARADISE

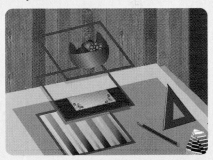

What is a layer?

A layer is like a transparent overlay over the photo. Layers can contain one or more objects, such as text, or adjustments you make to the photo. You can add multiple layers and combine, duplicate, and hide layers in an image. The *Teach Yourself VISUALLY Photoshop Elements 2* book is an excellent resource for more details on layers.

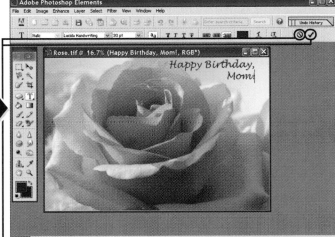

5 Type the text you want.

■ To start a blank line, press Enter.

6 Click ✓.

■ You can click ⊘ to cancel the text insertion.

■ Photoshop Elements adds the type on a separate layer.

ADD VERTICAL TEXT TO A PHOTO

You can add vertical text to a photo you want to use in a project such as a calendar or card. Or, you can add vertical text to fit the orientation of the photo.

© 2004 Charlotte K. Lowrie

ADD VERTICAL TEXT TO A PHOTO

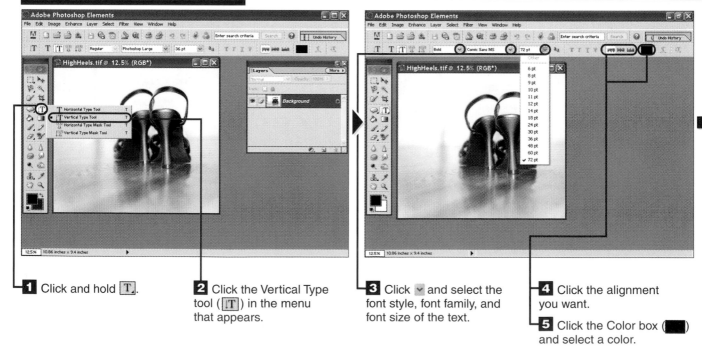

1 Click and hold T.

2 Click the Vertical Type tool (|T) in the menu that appears.

3 Click ⌄ and select the font style, font family, and font size of the text.

4 Click the alignment you want.

5 Click the Color box (▮) and select a color.

160

How can I stylize the text?

You can stylize the text in your image using the Free Transform command.

■1 Click the text layer in the **Layers** palette.

■2 Click **Image**.

■3 Click **Transform**.

■4 Click **Free Transform**.

■ Elements selects the text.

■5 Click a selection handle and drag.

■6 Click ☑ to apply the rotation.

■ Elements applies the transformation.

■6 Click and type the text you want.

■ Photoshop Elements inserts the text vertically.

SWITCH THE TEXT FROM VERTICAL TO HORIZONTAL

■1 Click the layer containing the vertical type you want to realign.

■2 Click the Change the Text Orientation button (🔲).

■ Photoshop Elements aligns the text horizontally.

EDIT TEXT

If you want to change
the text on a photo, you
can edit it in Photoshop
Elements.

EDIT TEXT

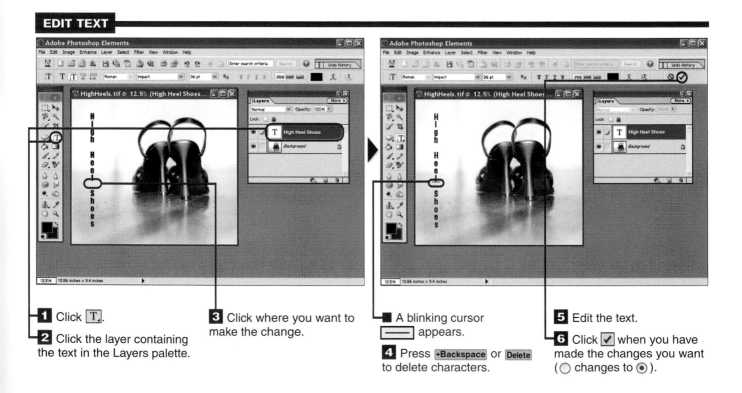

1 Click T.

2 Click the layer containing
the text in the Layers palette.

3 Click where you want to
make the change.

■ A blinking cursor
 ——— appears.

4 Press **+Backspace** or **Delete**
to delete characters.

5 Edit the text.

6 Click ✓ when you have
made the changes you want
(○ changes to ◉).

DELETE TEXT

If you want to remove
the text on a photo, you
can delete the layer that
contains the text in
Photoshop Elements.

DELETE TEXT

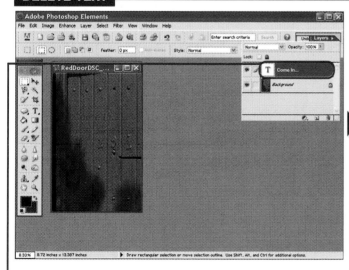

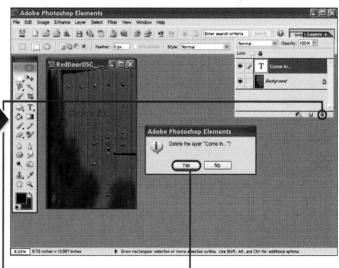

1 Click the layer that
contains the text you want
to delete.

2 Click 🗑.

■ Photoshop Elements asks
if you want to delete
the layer.

3 Click **Yes.**

■ Photoshop Elements
deletes the text layer.

ADD A TEXT EFFECT

Along with selecting the font style, size, and color, you can also stylize text using Text Effects.

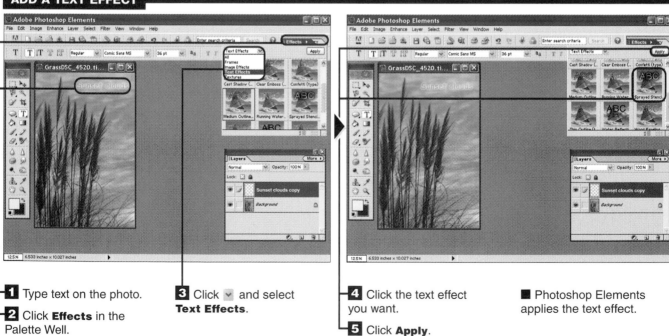

1 Type text on the photo.

2 Click **Effects** in the Palette Well.

3 Click ✓ and select **Text Effects**.

4 Click the text effect you want.

5 Click **Apply**.

■ Photoshop Elements applies the text effect.

ADD A LAYER STYLE TO A PHOTO

Photoshop Elements includes a variety of layer styles that you can apply to photos, including fog, snow, night-vision, and sun-faded effects.

ADD A LAYER STYLE TO A PHOTO

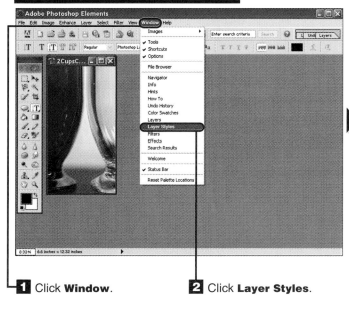

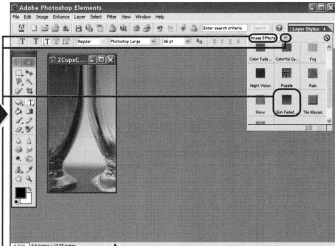

1 Click **Window**.

2 Click **Layer Styles**.

3 Click ⏷.

4 Click the layer style you want.

5 Click an effect.

■ This example uses the Sun Faded Image option in the Image Effects.

■ Photoshop Elements applies the layer style.

CREATE A DROP SHADOW

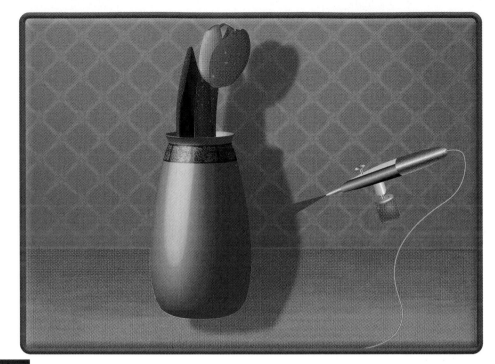

A drop shadow makes an item on a photo look raised from the background. You can use drop shadows for displaying photos on the Web.

CREATE A DROP SHADOW

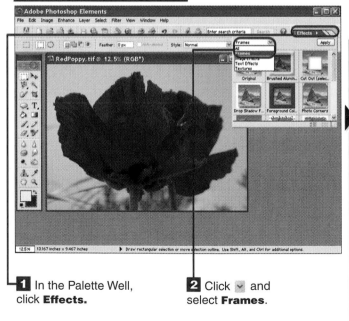

1 In the Palette Well, click **Effects**.

2 Click ⊡ and select **Frames**.

3 Click **Drop Shadow Frame**.

4 Click **Apply**.

■ Photoshop Elements creates a drop shadow.

■ To see the drop shadow, click and drag the window border to increase the window size.

ADD A FRAME

To give your photo a
finished look, especially
for display on the Web,
you can add a frame.

ADD A FRAME

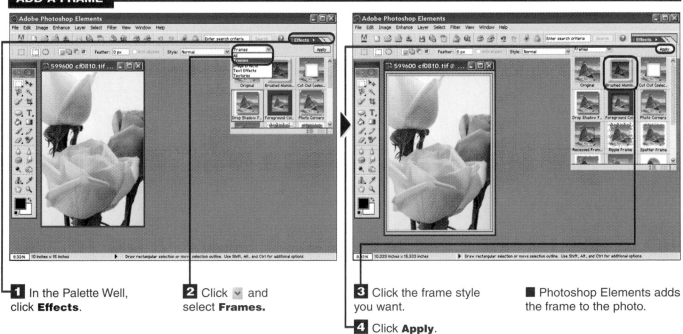

1 In the Palette Well,
click **Effects**.

2 Click ☑ and
select **Frames.**

3 Click the frame style
you want.

4 Click **Apply**.

■ Photoshop Elements adds
the frame to the photo.

USE SPECIAL EFFECT LIGHTING

You can enhance a photo by using special lighting effects in Photoshop Elements. For example, you can focus attention on a subject and change the overall lighting in the image by choosing the spotlight option.

CHANGE LIGHTING

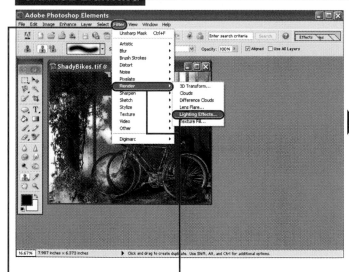

1 Click **Filter.**

2 Click **Render.**

3 Click **Lighting Effects.**

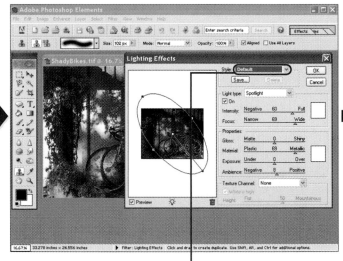

■ The Lighting Effects dialog box appears.

■ Photoshop Elements displays a small preview of the effect.

4 Click ∨ and select a lighting style.

What do the gloss and material options do?

In lighting effects, gloss refers to how much light reflects from the surface of the object. Shiny reflects a lot, while matte reflects a little. Material determines whether the light or the object on which the light shines reflects more light.

What do exposure and ambience do?

In lighting effects, exposure increases if you move the slider to the Over position, and decreases when you move the slider to the Under position. Ambience mixes the light as if it were from multiple light sources, such as fluorescent and natural light. Move the slider to the left to increase diffusion.

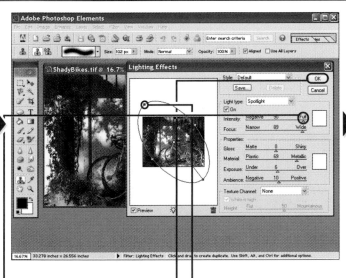

5 Drag ▲ to control the light intensity.

6 Click and drag the handles to adjust the shape and size of the lighting effect.

7 Click **OK**.

■ Photoshop Elements applies the lighting effects to the photo.

■ If you do not like the effects, click **Edit**, and then click **Undo Lighting Effects**.

CREATE A COMPOSITE PHOTO

You can superimpose all or parts of one or more photos onto another photo to create a composite image.

CREATE A COMPOSITE PHOTO

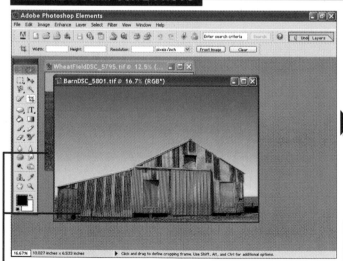

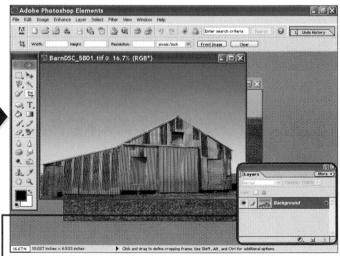

1 Open an image file.

2 Open the images you want to superimpose.

■ For best results, composite only a few images.

3 Click and drag the Layers palette from the Palette Well to the workspace.

■ Photoshop Elements displays the active photo in the Layers palette.

Does compositing photos increase file size?

The more pictures you composite, the larger the file size becomes. If both files are 1MB, and you combine them, the non-flattened image is 2MB. However, you can reduce the file size by choosing Flatten Image from the Layer menu. However, you cannot edit individual layers after flattening the image.

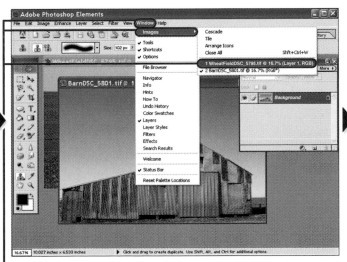

What kinds of pictures should I composite?

That depends on what you want to create. Photos that combine to tell a story, create a sequence, share symbolism, or are in some way related, work best.

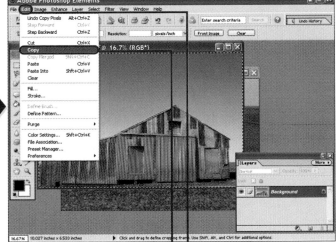

4 Click **Window**.

5 Click **Images**.

6 Click the filename of the photo you want to composite with the other photo.

■ You can scale photos before compositing them by clicking **Image, Resize,** and then **Scale**. Finally, click and drag the selection handles to decrease the size proportionally.

7 Click **Select**.

8 Click **Select All**.

9 Click **Edit**.

10 Click **Copy**.

CONTINUED

CREATE A COMPOSITE PHOTO

To learn more about compositing photos, check the Photoshop Elements Help topics.

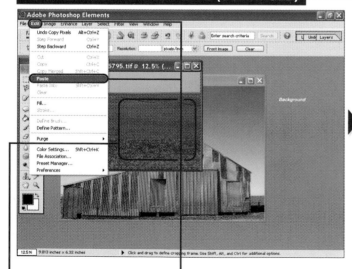

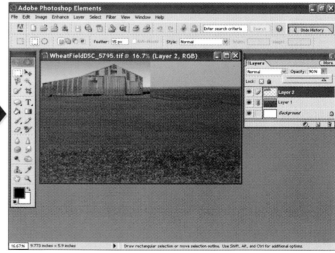

■ 11 Click the photo into which you want to paste the selection.

■ 12 Click **Edit**.

■ 13 Click **Paste**.

■ Photoshop Elements pastes the selection into the picture.

■ In this composite, the second picture was scaled to a smaller size.

172

Can I blend the second picture into the first?

You can use blending modes to merge the colors of the selected layer. Each blending option analyzes colors in the layers and adjusts them in different ways. For example, the Multiply mode darkens the colors when the selected layer overlaps layers below it. Color takes the active layer's colors and blends them with the details of the layers below it.

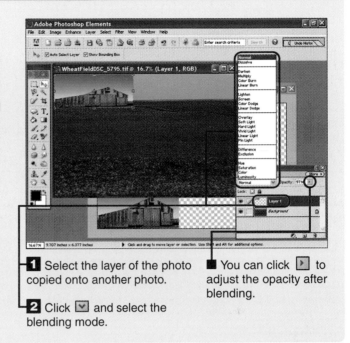

1 Select the layer of the photo copied onto another photo.

2 Click ▼ and select the blending mode.

■ You can click ▶ to adjust the opacity after blending.

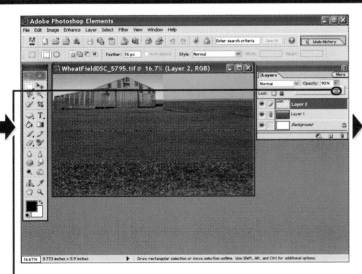

14 Drag ▲ to adjust how much of the second image shows through.

■ Dragging left reveals less of the second image. Dragging right reveals more of the second image.

■ Photoshop Elements changes the opacity of the photo.

■ After you click **Layer**, and then click **Flatten Image,** you can use the Clone Stamp tool to blend elements of the composite.

CREATE A PANORAMIC IMAGE

A panoramic image gives a sweeping view by combining several images. You can use the Photomerge feature to combine several images together into a panoramic image.

CREATE A PANORAMIC IMAGE

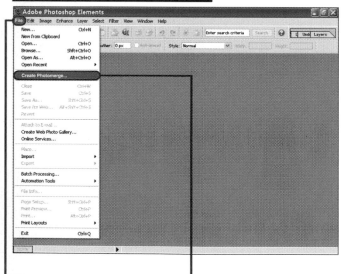

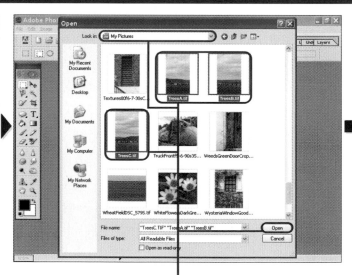

1 Click **File**.

2 Click **Create Photomerge**.

■ The Photomerge dialog box appears.

3 Click **Browse**.

■ The Open dialog box appears.

4 Click ⌄ and select the folder with the images you want to combine.

5 Press Shift and click the images you want to combine.

6 Click **Open**.

How can I take pictures that I can combine successfully?

To successfully merge photos, try these tips: Take pictures with a tripod and take each picture at the same height as the others. Avoid using lenses that cause distortion, such as very wide zoom settings and fisheye lenses. Include an overlap of 30 to 50 percent in each photo.

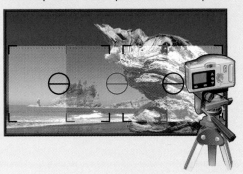

What if I did not follow the tips for shooting pictures so they combine easily?

In some cases, you can use the Clone tool to blend or disguise areas that do not match up precisely. Before cloning, magnify the photos to 200 percent to ensure the cloning is exact.

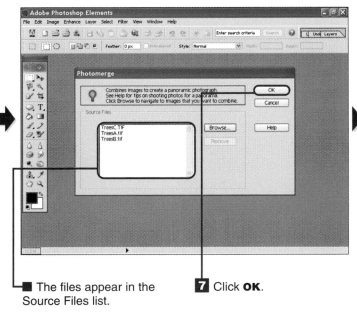

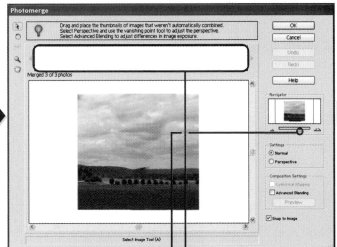

■ The files appear in the Source Files list.

7 Click **OK**.

■ Photoshop Elements combines the images into a single picture.

■ If Photoshop Elements cannot merge a picture, then it appears in the lightbox area.

■ To zoom the image, click and drag ▲ .

CONTINUED

CREATE A PANORAMIC IMAGE

You can align images in your panorama using the Photomerge dialog box.

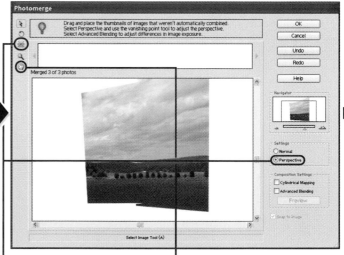

8 Click the Select Image tool (⟋).

■ If there is an image in the lightbox, then you can use the Select Image tool to click and drag it to the work area.

9 Click and drag a picture to line it up more precisely with the other pictures.

10 Click **Perspective** (○ changes to ◉).

11 To adjust perspective, click the Vanishing Point tool (⬚).

12 Click the picture.

■ Photoshop Elements adjusts the picture based on the point you click, shifting the image to create the correct perspective.

■ You can adjust placement of the entire panorama in the main window with the Hand tool 🖑.

What is Advanced Blending?

If pictures in the panorama show exposure differences, then you can use **Advanced Blending** in the Photomerge dialog box to adjust for exposure differences.

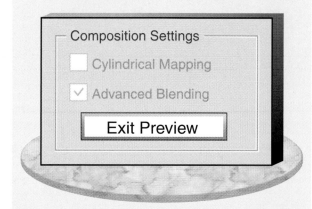

What does Snap to Image do?

If you place images that Photoshop Elements could not merge into the panorama, then you can click **Snap to Image** in the Photomerge dialog box to merge image edges.

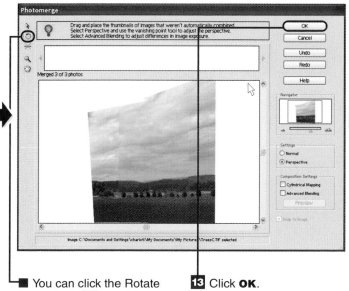

■ You can click the Rotate Image tool (⟳), and then click and drag to align unleveled pictures.

13 Click **OK**.

■ Photoshop Elements merges the images and opens the new panorama in a new image window.

■ You can click 🔲 to crop the final image.

■ You can blend seams with 🔄.

Note: See Chapter 10 to use the Clone Stamp tool, and Chapter 12 to crop an image.

DISTORT A PHOTO

Distortion can help after you correct for lens distortions, such as wide-angle lens distortion and keystoning. You can also use distortion to create unusual perspectives in your photos.

APPLY THE PINCH FILTER

1 Click **Filter**.

2 Click **Distort**.

3 Click **Pinch**.

■ The Pinch dialog box appears.

■ To see the overall effect, click 🔲 repeatedly to reduce the size of the preview.

4 Drag ⌂ to set the amount of the effect.

5 Click **OK**.

■ Photoshop Elements applies the filter.

Is there a way to create a fisheye lens effect in my image?

You can create a fisheye lens effect by using the Spherize filter. To adjust the amount of the distortion, click and drag △.

Can I apply distortion to part of a photo?

To apply distortion to part of a photo, you can select the part of the photo you want to distort, and then apply the filter. To select, click the Magnetic Lasso tool or the Selection Brush.

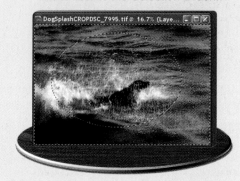

APPLY THE SHEAR FILTER FILTER

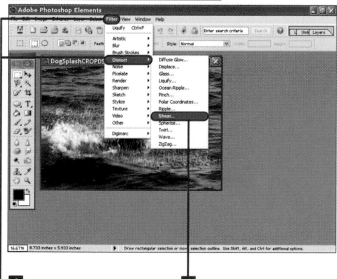

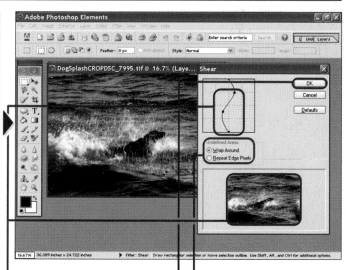

1 Click **Filter**.

2 Click **Distort**.

3 Click **Shear**.

■ The Shear dialog box appears.

4 Click and drag the coordinates to shape the Shear effect.

■ You can preview the effect here.

5 Click **Wrap Around** to wrap deleted pixels to the other side, or click **Repeat Edge Pixels** to fill in deleted pixels

6 Click **OK**.

■ Photoshop Elements applies the filter.

USE COLOR SELECTIVELY

If you want to make part of a photo stand out, such as an object against a background, then you can have only part of the photo in color and the rest in black and white.

1 Click the Brush tool (🖌).

2 Click ⊡ and select a brush type.

3 Click ▶ and select a brush size.

4 Click ▼ and select **Color**.

5 Click (🖌) the Set Foreground Color button to set black as the foreground color.

6 Click and drag to paint over areas you do not want in color.

■ Photoshop Elements removes color from the painted areas.

COMBINE EFFECTS

Combining effects enables you to completely transform a photo by giving it an entirely new look. In this example, you can create a high-contrast grayscale photo.

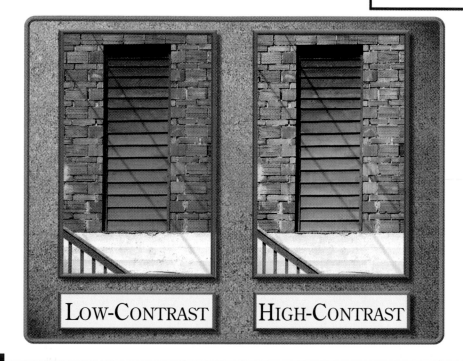

LOW-CONTRAST

HIGH-CONTRAST

COMBINE EFFECTS

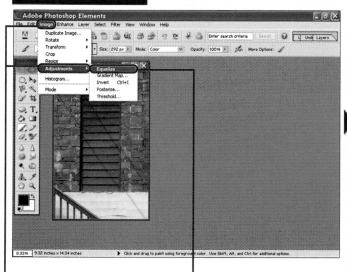

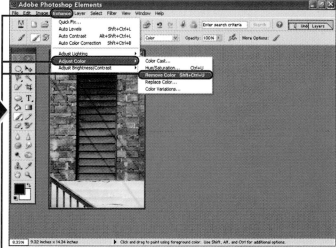

1 Click **Image**.

2 Click **Adjustments**.

3 Click **Equalize**.

■ Photoshop Elements evens out the brightness values of the picture.

4 Click **Enhance**.

5 Click **Adjust Color**.

6 Click **Remove Color**.

■ Photoshop Elements creates a high-contrast grayscale image.

■ You can apply additional effects to the image, such as a Sketch filter.

ADD MOTION BLUR TO A PHOTO

If you forgot to set a slow shutter speed, then you can add motion after taking your picture by using the Blur filter.

BLUR

LESS   MORE

ADD MOTION BLUR TO A PHOTO

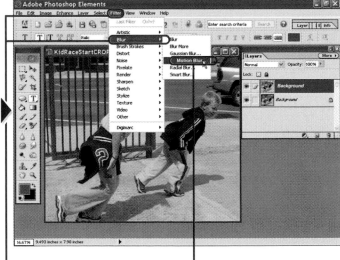

1 Drag the Layers palette from the Palette Well to the workspace.

2 Click **Layer**.

3 Click **Duplicate Layer**.

4 Type a name for the layer.

■ Photoshop Elements creates a duplicate layer and adds it to the Layers palette.

5 Click **Filter**.

6 Click **Blur**.

7 Click **Motion Blur**.

How do I control the blur direction?

Photoshop Elements shows the angle
of blur in the Motion Blur dialog box.
Select an angle that matches the
motion of the subject. For example, if
the subject is moving at a slight uphill
angle, then adjust the angle upward.

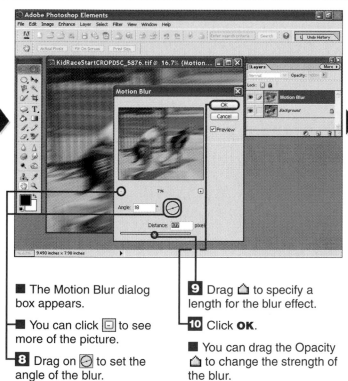

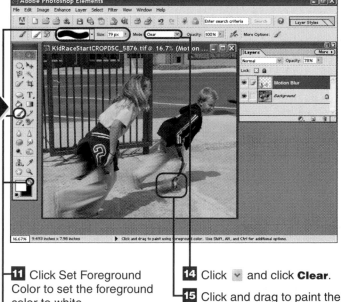

■ The Motion Blur dialog
box appears.

■ You can click □ to see
more of the picture.

8 Drag on ⊖ to set the
angle of the blur.

9 Drag △ to specify a
length for the blur effect.

10 Click **OK**.

■ You can drag the Opacity
△ to change the strength of
the blur.

11 Click Set Foreground
Color to set the foreground
color to white.

12 Click ✐.

13 Select the brush style
and size.

14 Click ▾ and click **Clear**.

15 Click and drag to paint the
areas where you do not want
to show a blur.

183

CREATE A CUSTOM VIGNETTE

To focus attention on an element within the photo, you can soften the focus of other elements in the photo using the Blur filter. You can also create a white or colored oval vignette around the subject.

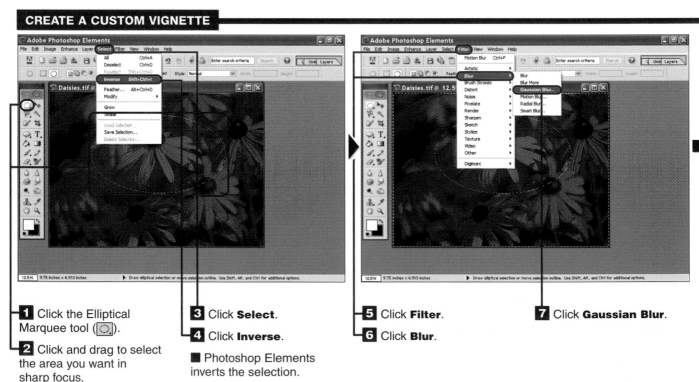

1 Click the Elliptical Marquee tool (⬭).

2 Click and drag to select the area you want in sharp focus.

3 Click **Select**.

4 Click **Inverse**.

■ Photoshop Elements inverts the selection.

5 Click **Filter**.

6 Click **Blur**.

7 Click **Gaussian Blur**.

184

How do I soften the vignette edges?

You can soften the edges by choosing a Feather value when you select the Elliptical Marquee tool. The larger the number, the softer the edges.

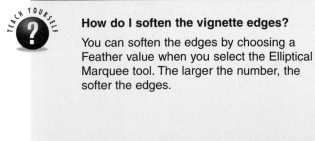

Feather: 15 px   ☑ Anti-aliased

Is the Gaussian Blur the only way to create a vignette?

You can use other blur filters, such as the Radial Blur filter, to create different effects. You should match the blur effect with the subject.

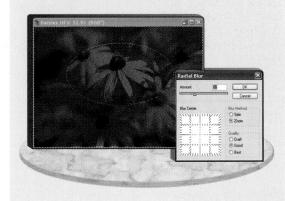

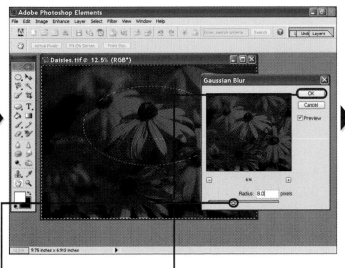

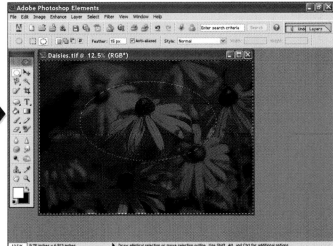

■ The Gaussian Blur dialog box appears.

8 Drag 🔺 to increase or decrease the number of dissimilar pixels that Photoshop Elements uses for the blur.

■ The larger the radius, the greater the blur.

9 Click **OK**.

■ Photoshop Elements applies the blur to the image.

■ If you do not like the effect, click **Edit**, and then click **Undo**.

ADD A QUICK VIGNETTE

For a classic photo look, you can use the Vignette effect in Photoshop Elements.

ADD A QUICK VIGNETTE

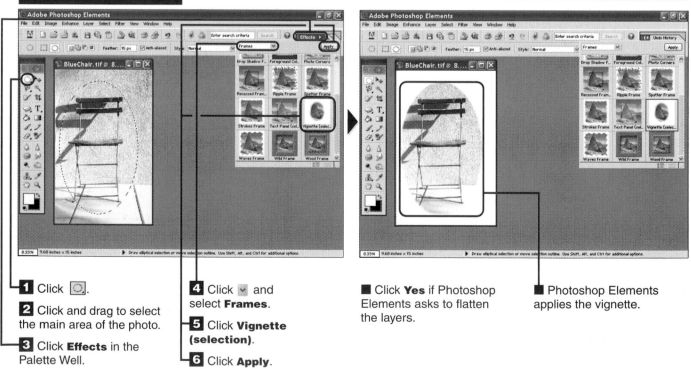

1 Click ◎.

2 Click and drag to select the main area of the photo.

3 Click **Effects** in the Palette Well.

4 Click ⌄ and select **Frames**.

5 Click **Vignette (selection)**.

6 Click **Apply**.

■ Click **Yes** if Photoshop Elements asks to flatten the layers.

■ Photoshop Elements applies the vignette.

For displaying images on
the Web, you can quickly
add a simulated matte
effect to photos in
Photoshop Elements.

ADD A QUICK MATTE EFFECT

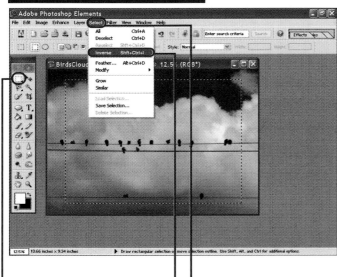

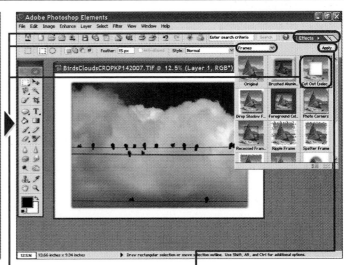

1 Click the Rectangular
Marquee tool (▦).

2 Click and drag to select
the main area of the photo.

3 Click **Select**.

4 Click **Inverse**.

■ Photoshop Elements
inverts the selection.

5 Click **Effects** in the
Palette Well.

6 Click ∨ and
select **Frames**.

7 Click **Cut Out**.

8 Click **Apply**.

■ Photoshop Elements
applies a white border with a
drop shadow to the photo.

ADD TEXTURE TO AN IMAGE

To make a photo resemble a painting on canvas or a watercolor painting, you can add textures, such as canvas and watercolor, using a Texture filter.

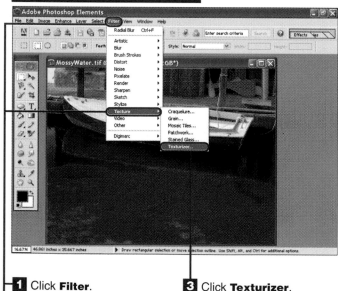

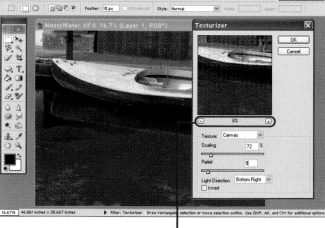

1 Click **Filter**.

2 Click **Texture**.

3 Click **Texturizer**.

■ The Texturizer dialog box appears.

■ You can click either ⊟ to zoom out or ⊞ to zoom in.

What does the Stained Glass filter do?

The Stained Glass filter converts areas of the photo into different solid-color shapes that resemble stained glass.

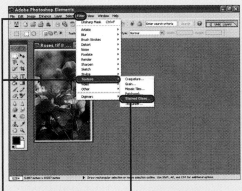

1 Click **Filter**.

2 Click **Texture**.

3 Click **Stained Glass**.

■ The Stained Glass dialog box appears.

4 Drag □ to change the size of cells and borders, and the shape of cells.

5 Click **OK**.

■ Elements applies the filter.

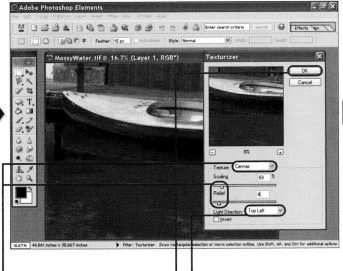

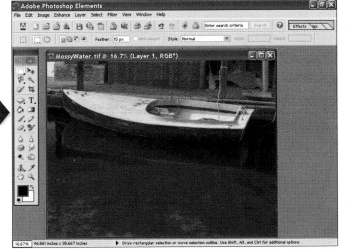

4 Click ☑ and select a texture.

5 Drag □ to control the scale and intensity of the texture.

6 Click ☑ and select a light direction.

7 Click **OK**.

■ Photoshop Elements applies the filter.

■ You can apply a texture to a separate layer, and then control the intensity using the Opacity control.

TINT A PHOTO

A standard photographic processing technique involves toning images to create a single overall hue. You can simulate a toned image in Photoshop Elements using a combination of tools.

TINT A PHOTO

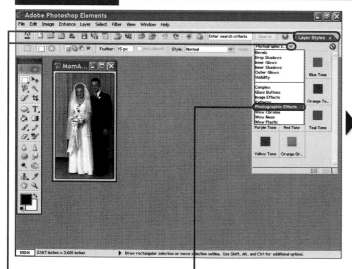

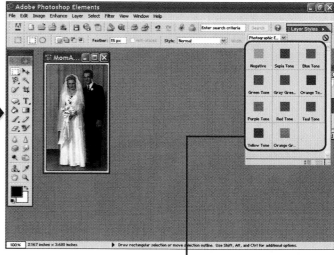

1 Click **Layer Styles** in the Palette Well.

2 Click ⊻.

3 Click **Photographic Effects**.

■ The Photographic Effects Layer Styles palette appears.

4 Click the tone you want.

■ Photoshop Elements applies the tone to the photo.

CREATE A SEPIA-TONE PHOTO

If you want to give a
photo a vintage look or
create a soft classic
toned effect, you can
apply a sepia-tone effect
in Photoshop Elements
using Layer Styles.

CREATE A SEPIA-TONE PHOTO

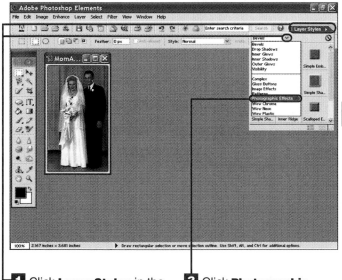

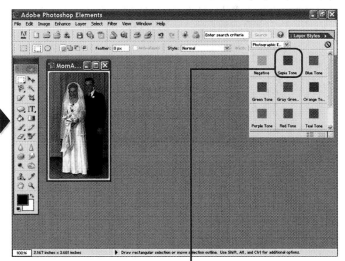

1 Click **Layer Styles** in the
Palette Well.

2 Click ⌄.

3 Click **Photographic
Effects**.

■ The Photographic Effects
Layer Styles palette appears.

4 Click **Sepia Tone.**

■ Photoshop Elements
applies the tint to the photo.

LIQUIFY A PHOTO

You can add a sense of
motion and softness
using the Photoshop
Elements Liquify filter.

LIQUIFY A PHOTO

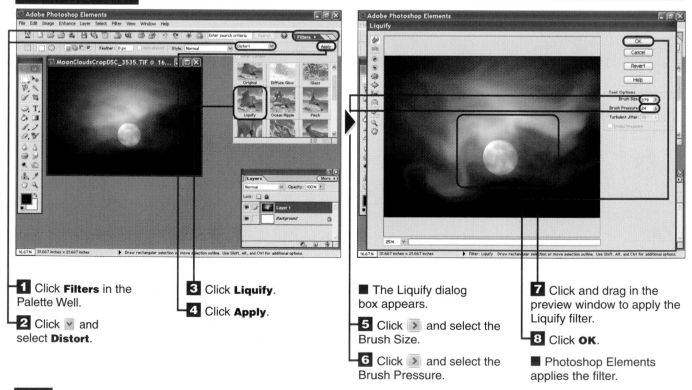

1 Click **Filters** in the
Palette Well.

2 Click ⌄ and
select **Distort**.

3 Click **Liquify**.

4 Click **Apply**.

■ The Liquify dialog
box appears.

5 Click ▶ and select the
Brush Size.

6 Click ▶ and select the
Brush Pressure.

7 Click and drag in the
preview window to apply the
Liquify filter.

8 Click **OK**.

■ Photoshop Elements
applies the filter.

192

ADD A GRADIENT TO A PHOTO

A gradient fades a color, or a gray, from light to dark or dark to light. Gradients can create interesting effects in photos.

ADD A GRADIENT TO A PHOTO

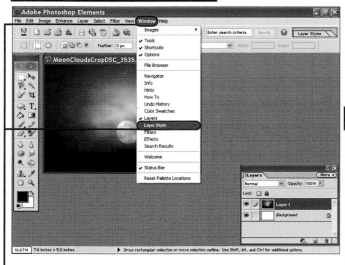

1 Click **Window**.

2 Click **Layer Styles**.

■ The Layer Styles palette appears.

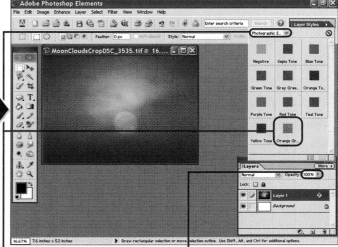

3 Click ⌄ and select **Photographic Effects**.

4 Click **Orange Gradient**.

■ Photoshop Elements applies the gradient to the active layer.

■ You can change the intensity of the gradient by lowering the opacity in the Layers palette.

CREATE A PHOTO COLLAGE

You can use the
Photomerge feature in
Photoshop Elements to
stitch several images
together into a photo
collage.

CREATE A PHOTO COLLAGE

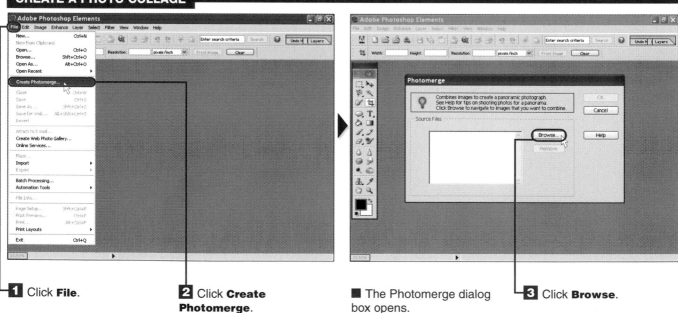

1 Click **File**.

2 Click **Create Photomerge**.

■ The Photomerge dialog box opens.

3 Click **Browse**.

194

TEACH YOURSELF ?

Can I add more photos to my collage from other folders?

Yes. In the Photomerge dialog box shown in step **7**, click the **Browse** button again and navigate to another folder from which you want to select files. You can also remove a file from the list by clicking the file and clicking the **Remove** button.

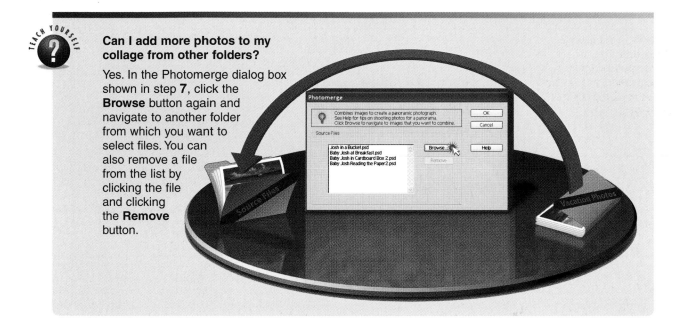

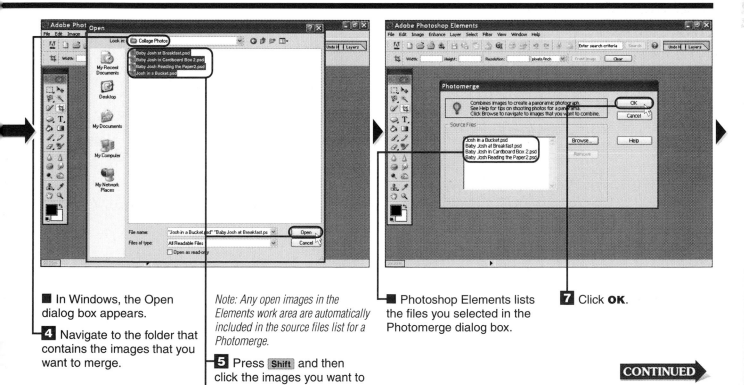

■ In Windows, the Open dialog box appears.

4 Navigate to the folder that contains the images that you want to merge.

Note: Any open images in the Elements work area are automatically included in the source files list for a Photomerge.

5 Press Shift and then click the images you want to select.

6 Click **Open**.

■ Photoshop Elements lists the files you selected in the Photomerge dialog box.

7 Click **OK**.

CONTINUED ▶

CREATE A PHOTO COLLAGE

The Photomerge dialog box allows you to interactively align the images that make up your collage.

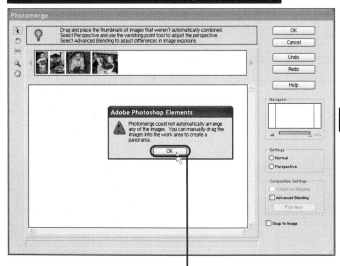

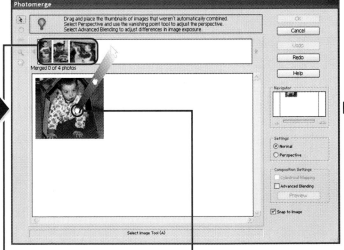

■ Because your photos are not part of a panoramic photo, Elements displays a warning box.

8 Click **OK**.

■ Thumbnails of the selected images appear in a lightbox area.

9 Click and drag an image from the lightbox to the work area.

196

How can I rotate a photo in my collage?

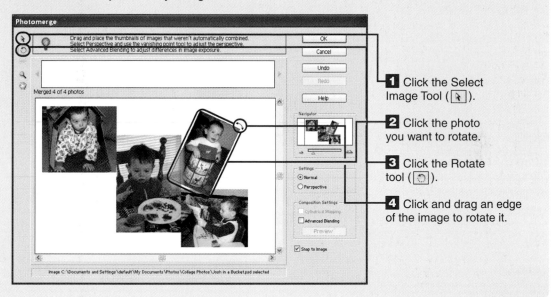

Photomerge

Drag and place the thumbnails of images that weren't automatically combined.
Select Perspective and use the vanishing point tool to adjust the perspective.
Select Advanced Blending to adjust differences in image exposure.

Merged 4 of 4 photos

OK
Cancel
Undo
Redo
Help

Navigator

Settings
○ Normal
○ Perspective

Composition Settings
☐ Cylindrical Mapping
☐ Advanced Blending
Preview

☑ Snap to Image

Image C:\Documents and Settings\default\My Documents\Photos\Collage Photos\Josh in a Bucket.psd selected

1 Click the Select
Image Tool (⬉).

2 Click the photo
you want to rotate.

3 Click the Rotate
tool (↻).

4 Click and drag an edge
of the image to rotate it.

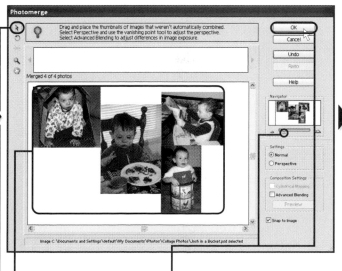

10 Click and drag the
remaining images from the
lightbox to the work area to
create a collage
arrangement.

■ You can click the Select
Image Tool (⬉), and then
click and drag an image to
move it around the screen.

■ You can zoom in and out
by adjusting the Navigator
slider (△).

11 Click **OK**.

■ Photoshop Elements
merges the images and
opens the new collage in
a new image window.

*Note: To save the collage, see
Chapter 1.*

PAINT WITH THE PAINT BUCKET TOOL

You can fill areas in your image with solid color using the Paint Bucket tool. You can use this technique to change the color of clothes, eyes, the sky, backgrounds, and more. When you apply the Paint Bucket tool, it affects adjacent pixels in the image. You can set the Paint Bucket's Tolerance value to determine what range of colors the paint bucket affects when applied to the image.

PAINT WITH THE PAINT BUCKET TOOL

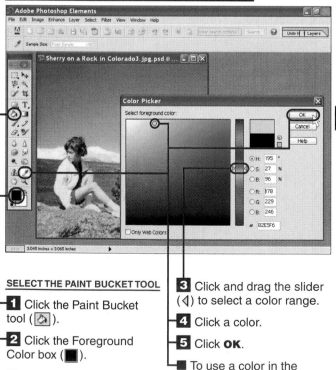

SELECT THE PAINT BUCKET TOOL

1 Click the Paint Bucket tool (⬚).

2 Click the Foreground Color box (■).

■ The Color Picker dialog box opens.

3 Click and drag the slider (◁) to select a color range.

4 Click a color.

5 Click **OK**.

■ To use a color in the photo, click 🖉, and then click a color in the photo.

SET THE TOLERANCE

6 Type a Tolerance value from 0 to 255.

7 Click inside the image.

■ Elements fills an area of the image with the foreground color.

How can I reset a tool to the default settings?

Click on the tool's icon on the far left side of the Options bar and select **Reset Tool** from the menu that appears.

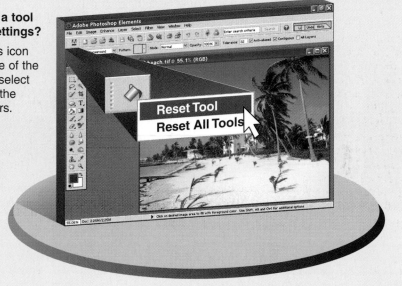

SET PAINT OPACITY

8 To fill an area with a semitransparent color, as shown in this example, type a percentage value of less than 100 in the Opacity field.

■ Elements fills an area with see-through paint.

CONSTRAIN THE COLOR

9 To constrain where you apply the color, make a selection before following steps **1** to **7** and clicking to apply the paint color.

■ The fill effect stays within the boundary of the selection.

CHAPTER 12

Crop, Size, and Sharpen Photos

To make the most of photos that you display on the Web, print, or use in projects, you can crop, size, and sharpen photos so they look their best.

WHY CROP, SIZE, AND SHARPEN PHOTOS?

The last steps in the digital workflow include cropping, sizing, and sharpening photos. Saving these steps for last ensures that photos look their best for each medium in which you use them.

Crop for Resolution and Composition

Cropping, or removing portions of a photo, can enhance the composition of a photo, but it also affects the overall resolution of the image. The more you crop, the smaller the file, and the smaller the file, the smaller the print you can make. Cropping judiciously keeps resolution high while, improving composition.

Sizing Photos

Like cropping, sizing photos affects the resolution, depending on the way you choose to resize photos. You can resize and set photos to lower resolutions that you want to display on the Web, send in e-mails, or use in presentations without affecting viewing quality. If you want to print a photo, then you can set sizing options to retain the highest resolution.

Sharpen Photos

Many digital images inherently look soft, or lack crisp details. You can use Photoshop Elements to increase the sharpness of your images. The sharpen settings vary, depending on how you use the photo. With small photos you use on the Web or in e-mail, you use different sharpen settings than for photos you print.

Why Not Sharpen Once and Use Many Times?

If you size and sharpen a photo to print at 8 by 10 inches and size it down for Web use, then the resized photo looks oversharpened, as shown here. If you size and sharpen a photo for the Web and later size it up for printing, then it produces a very low-quality print. Instead, make copies that you can size and sharpen for each specific use.

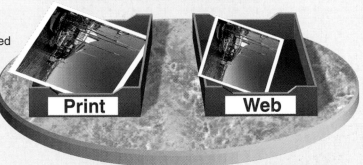

Keep Digital Negatives

Always keep the original digital file, or the digital negative, untouched. If anything goes wrong, then you can go back to the original file and begin again.

CROP A PHOTO

Using the Crop tool, you can crop your photo precisely where you want. This section describes the basic crop feature in Photoshop Elements.

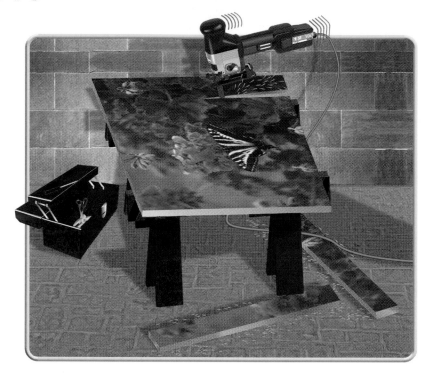

CROP A PHOTO

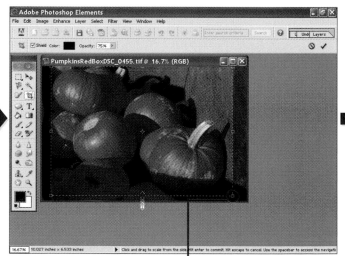

1 Click the Crop tool ().

2 Click and drag the cursor to select the area you want to keep.

■ Elements displays a screen over the areas that will be cropped.

■ Click and drag a corner handle to increase or decrease the crop size.

■ Click and drag within the crop boundary to move the crop without resizing it.

What should I know before I crop an image?

The most important consideration is how you plan to use the photo. If you want to print the photo, then crop only what you find distracting or unnecessary. Judicious cropping helps you retain the larger file sizes and resolution you need to make enlargements.

What should I know about in-camera cropping?

You achieve the best results if you crop when you take the picture. During shooting, you can change scene elements or move closer to fill the frame. The resulting image needs little or no cropping, and you retain full image size or resolution so you can print enlargements.

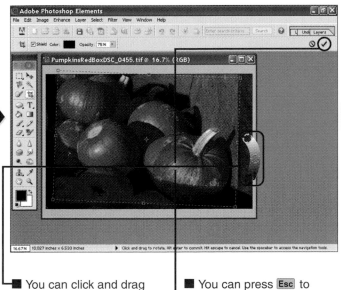

■ You can click and drag outside the crop boundary to rotate the photo.

■ You can press Esc to cancel the crop.

3 Click ✔ to crop the photo.

■ Elements crops the image.

■ If you do not like the cropped picture, click the Step Backward button (🔲).

CROP TO A SPECIFIC SIZE FOR PRINTING

Using the Crop tool, you can crop to a specific size. Use this technique to create a specific print size, such as 8 by 10 inches or 5 by 7 inches.

CROP TO A SPECIFIC SIZE FOR PRINTING

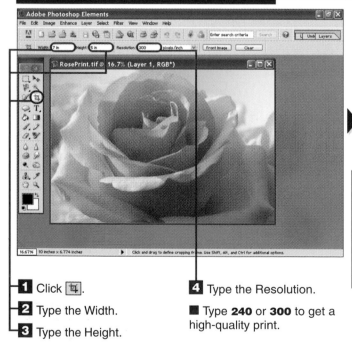

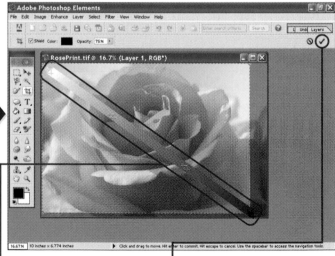

1 Click 🔲.

2 Type the Width.

3 Type the Height.

4 Type the Resolution.

■ Type **240** or **300** to get a high-quality print.

5 Click and drag to select the image area you want to keep.

■ Elements constrains the crop to the specified dimensions.

6 Click ✓ to crop the photo.

You can simultaneously crop and straighten a crooked photo in Photoshop Elements. This technique is most effective for images that were slightly rotated on the scanning bed during scanning.

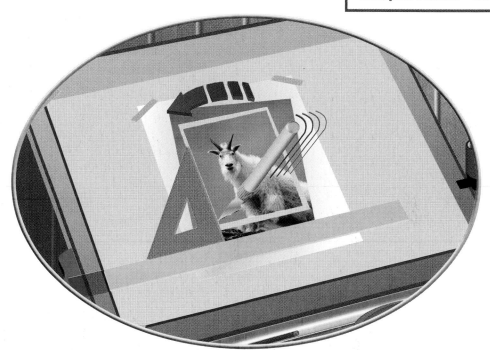

STRAIGHTEN AND CROP A PHOTO

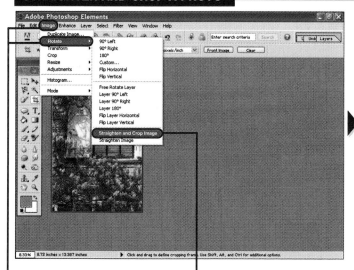

1 Click **Image**.

2 Click **Rotate**.

3 Click **Straighten and Crop Image**.

■ Elements rotates and crops the image.

■ If you do not like the results, click **Edit**, and then click **Undo Straighten and Crop Image**.

CROP WITH SPACE FOR TEXT

If you want to add a photo title or caption, but you do not want to type the text within the photo, then you can crop and add space around the border to type text. You can also use the extra space as a photo border.

CROP WITH SPACE FOR TEXT

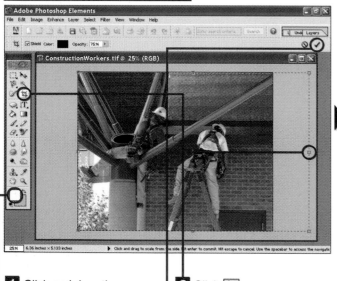

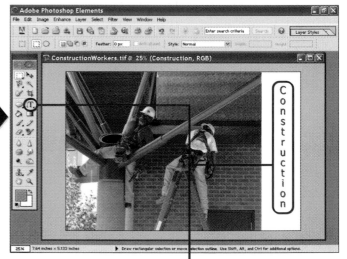

1 Click and drag the window border to increase the area around the photo.

2 Click here to set the foreground color to white.

3 Click ⛏.

4 Click and drag to crop.

5 Click and drag a crop handle ☐ outside the picture area.

6 Click ✓.

■ Elements crops the photo and adds space.

■ You can type text in the white space using the Horizontal or Vertical Type tool (T,).

If you do not care about
a specific crop size, and
you just want to quickly
crop a photo, then you
can use this technique.

CROP WITHOUT THE CROP TOOL

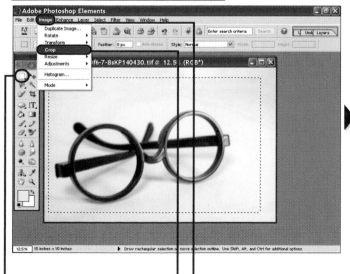

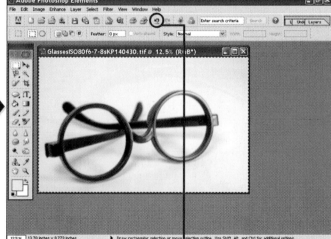

1 Click the Rectangular
Marquee tool (⬚).

2 Click and drag where you
want the crop.

3 Click **Image**.

4 Click **Crop**.

■ Elements crops the photo.

■ If you do not like the
cropped picture, click the
Step Backward button (◻).

DETERMINE SIZE BY PRINT RESOLUTION

For high-quality prints, you can set the image resolution. When you set the resolution, Photoshop Elements shows you the largest size at which you can print the photo at that resolution. Common printing resolutions are 240 dpi and 300 dpi.

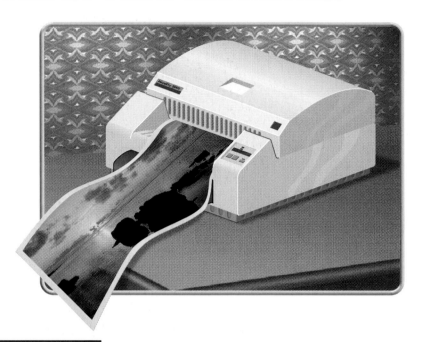

DETERMINE SIZE BY PRINT RESOLUTION

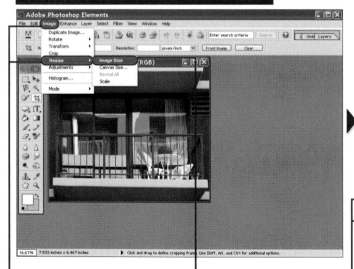

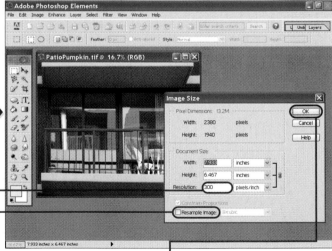

1 Click **Image**.

2 Click **Resize**.

3 Click **Image Size**.

■ The Image Size dialog box appears.

4 Click here to turn off image resampling (☑ changes to ☐).

5 Type **240** or **300** to set printer resolution.

■ You can type the specific printer resolution if it is different from 240 or 300 dpi.

■ The dimensions show the maximum printing size at the specified resolution.

Note: For digital photos, turn off Resample Image. For high-resolution scanned photos, turn on Resample Image.

6 Click **OK** to apply the new size.

If setting the print resolution does not produce an image size that fits the printing paper you use, then you can set the image width or height to fit within the paper dimensions. This technique works if you do not care whether the picture fits the page exactly.

SIZE A DIGITAL PHOTO TO A PAGE SIZE

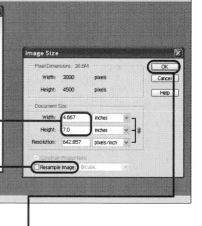

1 Click **Image**.

2 Click **Resize**.

3 Click **Image Size**.

■ The Image Size dialog box appears.

4 Click here to turn off image resampling (☑ changes to ☐).

5 Type the Width or type a Height.

■ The width or height dimension should match the printable area of the printer.

■ Elements automatically adjusts the other dimension proportionally and adjusts the resolution.

6 Click **OK** to resize the image.

SIZE A DIGITAL PHOTO FOR ONLINE USE

For online display, you can size pictures smaller, so that they quickly upload to a Web site or are small enough to send in e-mail.

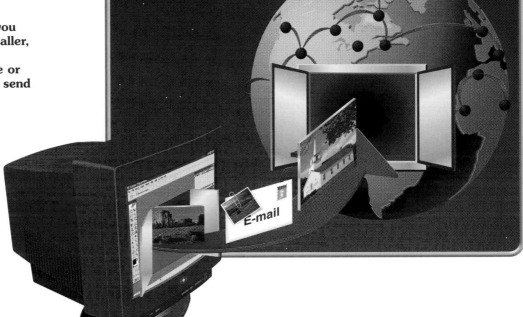

SIZE A DIGITAL PHOTO FOR ONLINE USE

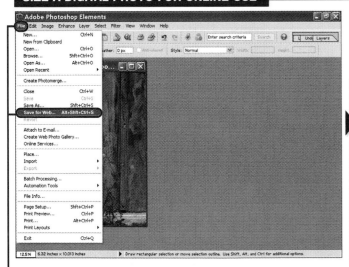

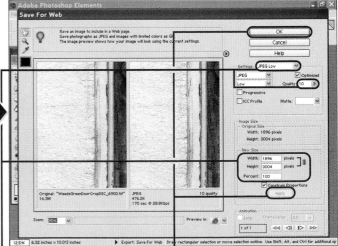

1 Click **File**.

2 Click **Save for Web**.

■ The Save For Web dialog box appears.

3 Click ▾ and select optimization and quality settings.

4 Type the Width or Height, or type a percentage.

5 Click **Apply**.

6 Click **OK**.

Which file format should I choose for online photos?

In general, JPEG format is a good choice for continuous-tone files, such as photos, because it preserves color, brightness, and hues. JPEG compresses files to reduce size by discarding some of the data. You can view the results of compression in the Save For Web dialog box samples.

What if my file contains text and solid colors?

If your file contains text and solid colors, then consider saving in GIF format. GIF format preserves the sharpness of text, while effectively preserving color when the file is compressed, unless you optimize a 24-bit image as an 8-bit GIF. If your file includes animation, then you can only save the file in GIF format.

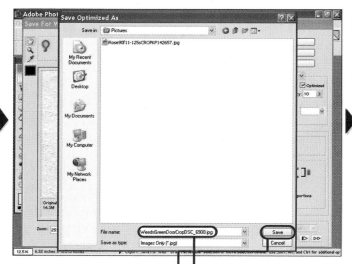

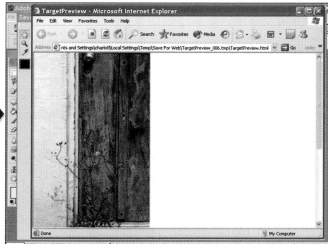

■ The Save Optimized As dialog box appears.

7 Type a filename.

8 Click **Save**.

PREVIEW AN ONLINE PICTURE

9 Click the Preview In: ⌄ in the Save For Web dialog box.

10 Select a browser.

■ Elements displays the picture in the Web browser.

SHARPEN A PHOTO FOR PRINTING

Before printing, you can increase the appearance of sharpness in a digital photo. The Unsharp Mask filter finds edges in the picture and increases the edge contrast so that the picture appears sharp.

SHARPEN A PHOTO FOR PRINTING

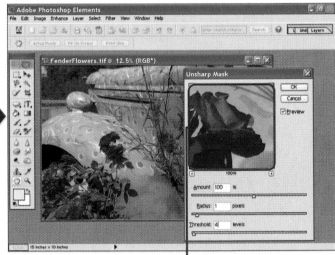

1 Open a photo that you sized or cropped for printing.

2 Click **Filter**.

3 Click **Sharpen**.

4 Click **Unsharp Mask**.

■ The Unsharp Mask dialog box appears.

■ Click inside the preview area and drag to move around the picture.

How much sharpening is too much?

To sharpen effectively, aim for a photo that looks pleasingly sharp but stops short of being oversharpened — having a glowing appearance to the edges. You can intentionally choose high settings and print the picture to see what oversharpening does to a photo.

What values should I select?

As a starting point for a high-resolution photo, start with moderate settings. If the image needs additional sharpening, then you can increase the settings.

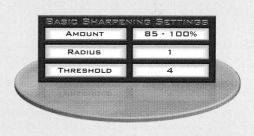

BASIC SHARPENING SETTINGS	
AMOUNT	85 - 100%
RADIUS	1
THRESHOLD	4

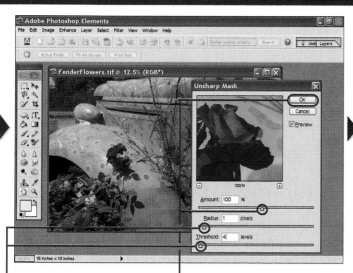

5 Drag ⌂ to set the number of edge pixels to sharpen.

6 Drag ⌂ to determine how different edge pixels must be before they are considered edge pixels.

Note: A value of zero sharpens all pixels.

7 Drag ⌂ to determine how much contrast Elements applies to the edges.

8 Click **OK**.

■ Elements sharpens the photo.

Note: Sharpening appears stronger on the screen than it does in the printed photo.

■ If the photo appears to have been oversharpened, click **2** to undo the sharpening.

SHARPEN A PHOTO FOR ONLINE USE

Because online photos are smaller and are a lower resolution than printed photos, you can use different sharpen settings, although the technique for sharpening is the same.

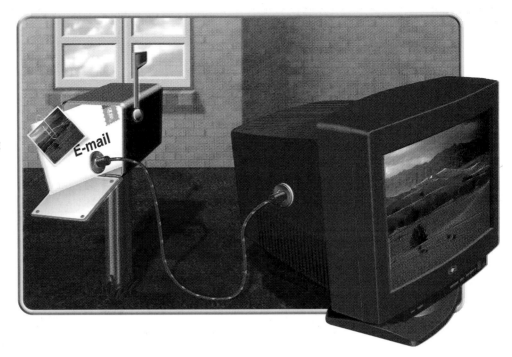

SHARPEN A PHOTO FOR ONLINE USE

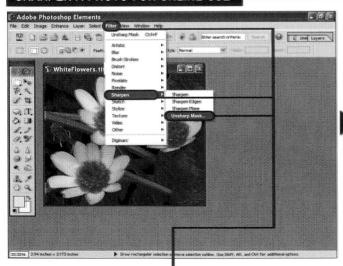

1 Open a picture you sized for online use.

2 Click **Filter**.

3 Click **Sharpen**.

4 Click **Unsharp Mask**.

■ The Unsharp Mask dialog box appears.

■ Click in the preview area and drag to move around the picture.

What magnification should I use to view my image to sharpen it?

You achieve better results if you view a photo at 100 percent magnification before you sharpen the photo. To zoom in, click  and watch the title bar until it displays 100%.

Will sharpening make a blurry picture sharp?

Depending on the amount of blur or soft focus, sharpening can help. You can set the Threshold value higher for soft subjects. However, keep in mind that the Sharpen filter does not produce photos as sharp as photos taken with a crisp focus.

5 Drag to set the number of edge pixels to sharpen.

6 Drag to determine how different edge pixels must be before they are considered edge pixels.

Note: A value of zero sharpens all pixels.

7 Drag to determine how much contrast Elements applies to the edges.

8 Click **OK**.

■ Elements sharpens the photo.

CONVERT FILE TYPES

You can convert all the image files in a folder to a specific file type. You may find this useful if you want to post a number of pictures on the Web and need the images in a Web file format such as GIF or JPEG.

Before you can begin, you need to create a source folder and a destination folder for your images. To work with folders, see your specific operating system's documentation. To open Elements, see Chapter 1.

CONVERT FILE TYPES

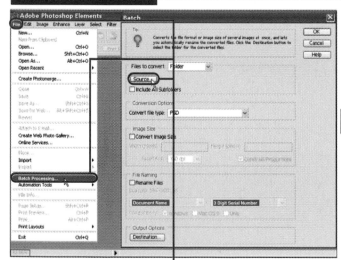

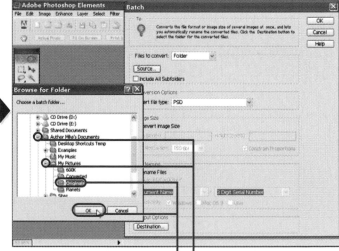

1 Place the images you want to convert into a source folder.

2 Create an empty destination folder in which to save your converted files.

3 Click **File**.

4 Click **Batch Processing**.

■ The Batch dialog box opens.

5 Click **Source**.

■ The Browse for Folder dialog box appears.

6 Click ⊞ to open folders.

7 Click the folder containing your images.

8 Click **OK**.

How do I rename the image files that I convert?

You can rename files using settings in the Batch dialog box:

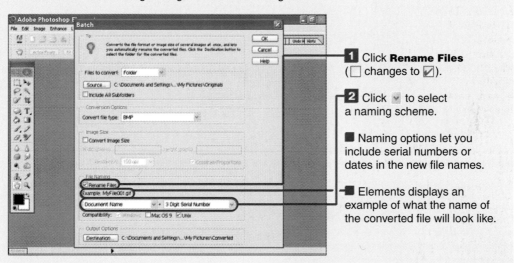

1 Click **Rename Files**
(☐ changes to ☑).

2 Click ⌄ to select
a naming scheme.

■ Naming options let you
include serial numbers or
dates in the new file names.

■ Elements displays an
example of what the name of
the converted file will look like.

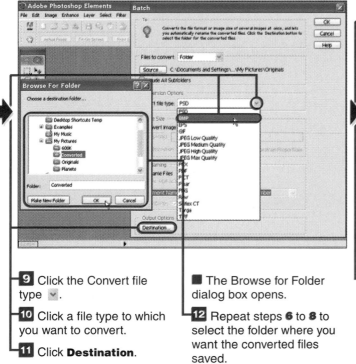

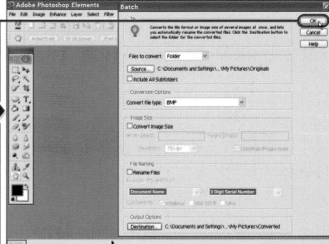

9 Click the Convert file
type ⌄.

10 Click a file type to which
you want to convert.

11 Click **Destination**.

■ The Browse for Folder
dialog box opens.

12 Repeat steps **6** to **8** to
select the folder where you
want the converted files
saved.

13 Click **OK**.

■ Elements cycles through
the image files in the source
folder.

■ Elements converts the
image files and saves the
new versions in the
destination folder.

CONVERT IMAGE SIZES

You can resize all the image files in a folder to specific dimensions. You may find this useful if you want to quickly convert a number of large files from a digital camera to smaller versions that you can store and view more efficiently.

Before you can begin, you need to create a source folder and a destination folder for your images. To work with folders, see your specific operating system's documentation. To open Elements, see Chapter 1.

CONVERT IMAGE SIZES

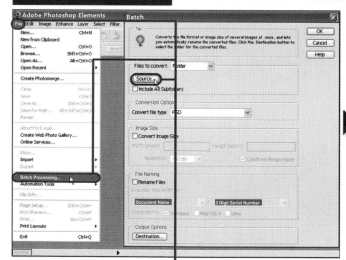

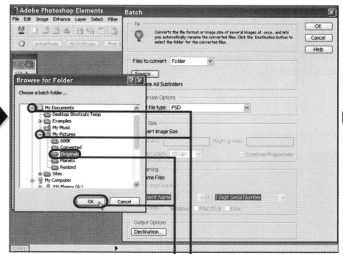

1 Place the images you want to resize into a source folder.

2 Create an empty destination folder in which to save your resized files.

3 Click **File**.

4 Click **Batch Processing**.

■ The Batch dialog box opens.

5 Click **Source**.

■ The Browse for Folder dialog box opens.

6 Click ⊞ to open folders.

7 Click the folder containing your images.

8 Click **OK**.

Can I batch process files that I currently have open in Elements?

Yes. In the Batch dialog box, just click the Files to covert ☑ and select **Opened Files**. Elements saves the processed files to the destination folder.

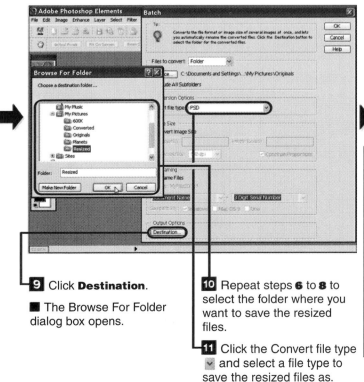

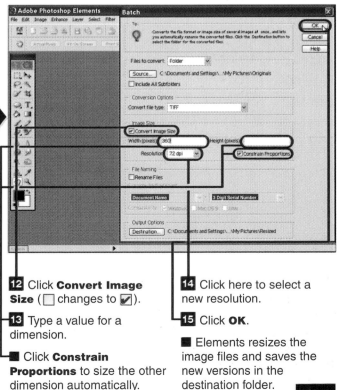

9 Click **Destination**.

■ The Browse For Folder dialog box opens.

10 Repeat steps **6** to **8** to select the folder where you want to save the resized files.

11 Click the Convert file type ☑ and select a file type to save the resized files as.

12 Click **Convert Image Size** (☐ changes to ☑).

13 Type a value for a dimension.

■ Click **Constrain Proportions** to size the other dimension automatically.

14 Click here to select a new resolution.

15 Click **OK**.

■ Elements resizes the image files and saves the new versions in the destination folder.

Jack's First Game

Photography Vol. 1
Photography Vol. 2
Photography Vol. 3

CHAPTER 13

Print Photos

Now that you have digital pictures, how do you print them? This chapter introduces the options for printing digital photos with a local or online photo lab service or at home.

UNDERSTANDING RESOLUTION

One step in achieving high-quality prints is to understand the basics of print resolution and how it relates to image resolution.

PPI and DPI

PPI and DPI are two different measurements of resolution. You measure image resolution by the number of pixels the image contains per inch — called *pixels per inch,* or ppi. You measure printer resolution by the number of dots it prints per inch — called *dots per inch,* or dpi.

PPI and Photo Size

The number of pixels in your image determines the maximum size at which you can print the photo. Printers typically print multiple dots for each pixel in an picture. If you try to print a large photo from a file that does not contain enough pixels, then the photo is *pixelated,* or displays jagged edges.

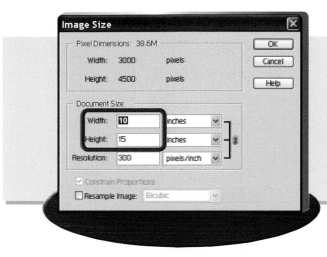

Print Size

An image resolution of 300 dpi or 240 dpi provides high-quality prints. You can determine how large you can print a picture at 300 dpi, by typing **300** in the resolution field, in the Image Size dialog box. You can turn on the Constrain Proportions option, and look at the dimensions in the Document Size box.

Calculate Print Size by Resolution

You can calculate print size. To print a 5" x 7"-inch image, at 300 ppi, you multiply 5 x 300 pixels, and then multiply 7 x 300 pixels for 1500 x 2100 pixels, respectively. To print a 5 x 7-inch print, your camera should to produce images measuring 1500 x 2100 pixels.

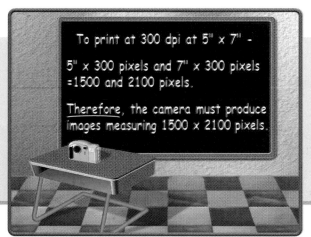

To print at 300 dpi at 5" x 7" -

5" x 300 pixels and 7" x 300 pixels =1500 and 2100 pixels.

Therefore, the camera must produce images measuring 1500 x 2100 pixels.

To calculate if your camera will produce a 5" x 7" print -

Image width x height in pixels: 1500 x 2100, or 3,150,000 or 3.15 million

3.15 million = the camera megapixel rating needed to print a 5" x 7" print at 300 dpi.

Calculate Print Size by Camera Resolution

To determine if your camera produces images that you can print at a 5" x 7"-inch size, multiply the image width by the height in pixels. For example, 1500 pixels multiplied by 2100 pixels equals 3,150,000 or 3.15 million pixels. 3.15 in millions roughly equals the camera megapixel rating, or number, required for a 5" x 7"-inch print at 300 dpi.

DIGITAL PHOTO PRINTING OPTIONS

Digital photography offers more options for getting good prints than ever before. You can learn about different options, as well as the advantages and disadvantages of each option.

Key Considerations

You can print digital pictures at home on your photo printer, at an online commercial service, at a kiosk, or at a traditional photo lab. Whichever option you choose, some of the key factors to consider include print quality, print longevity, turnaround time, cost per print, and convenience.

Print on a Home Photo Printer

For approximately $100 to $200, you can buy a five- to six-color photo printer that produces prints up to 8 by 10 inches or larger. Some printers print from your computer or directly from your memory card. Paper and ink costs vary, For example, an 8" x 10"-inch print costs between 50 cents and $1 depending, on the quality of paper.

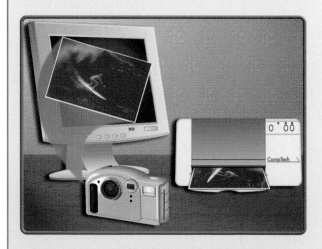

Advantages and Disadvantages

Home printers offer a fast setup, sharp and colorful prints, and the instant gratification that digital photography offers. However, if you want an exact color match between the onscreen image and the printed image, then color management can be inconvenient. Color management includes processing images in a consistent color space, calibrating your monitor often, and ensuring that you have the appropriate and current printer profiles. Also, some photos can fade within a few months.

Print at a Kiosk or a Photo Lab

You can print pictures at photo kiosks, located in photo stores and shopping centers, or at traditional photo labs. Print sizes range from 3 by 5 inches to 8 by 10 inches, with prices averaging 40 cents for a 4" x 6"-inch print — enlargements often cost disproportionately more. Print life is comparable to film prints.

Advantages and Disadvantages

Kiosks offer convenient photo printing at competitive prices. As with film, you take your memory card into a store to have prints made. Not all kiosks accept all types of memory cards. Some kiosks offer basic image-editing features. Unless your camera produces picture-perfect images that need no cropping, you may want to first edit images on the computer.

Print at an Online Commercial Photo Lab

You can upload pictures to Web sites that offer commercial photo printing. Most sites offer free online photo albums where you can share pictures with family and friends. You can order prints and novelty items, including photo t-shirts, calendars, and cards that are delivered to your door. Prices currently range from 30 to 50 cents for 4" x 6"-inch prints.

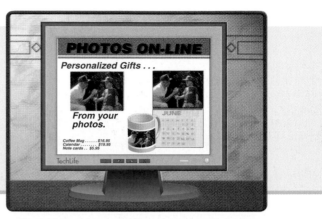

Advantages and Disadvantages

With the convenience of online print services, you can easily obtain long-life prints and other products. Some sites require you to download an upload tool to your computer. Other sites require a paid subscription to the service. Print quality can vary widely, so it pays to obtain prints from several services and compare the results.

Evaluate and Test First

With digital pictures, you can take advantage of any of the options discussed earlier. You can also use various options on an as-needed basis. If you decide to use a commercial service, try several services first and evaluate the print results. For most printing, you can use your home printer. If you are on vacation, then you can use a local kiosk. And if you want professional-quality enlargements, then you can use a commercial photo lab.

Get the Best Prints

Regardless of where and how you print your pictures, you get the best results by starting with a high-resolution file. To get a high-resolution file, set your camera to the highest resolution setting. This ensures that the file size is large enough to print high-quality photos and enlargements.

Crop with Restraint

Because cropping reduces the overall file size, use restraint when cropping photos. The more you crop, the smaller the file becomes, and the smaller the print you can make from the file.

Choosing Pictures for Enlargements

When you choose a picture for enlargement, look for pictures that have a high enough resolution for the size you want to enlarge it to, and pictures that display great color, strong composition, and good contrast. Then spend extra time editing the image carefully, and make test prints to check the results before printing the enlargement.

CHOOSE A PHOTO PRINTER

Choosing a photo printer can be educational and fun. Learn what to look for in a printer so that you can print high-quality photos at home.

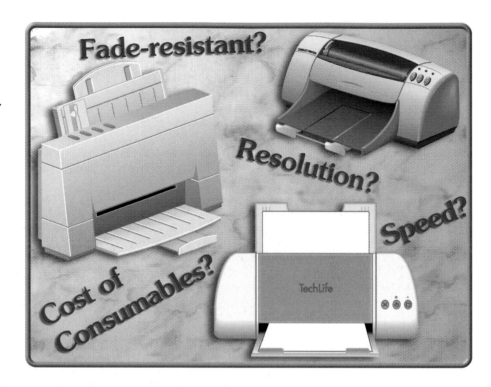

Know What to Look for in a Printer

When you shop for photo printers, look for resolution, print quality, cost of consumables, including ink and paper, and the length of print life, or how long you can display a print without noticeable fading.

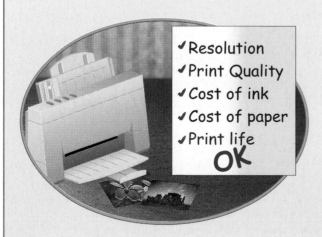

Choose a Printer

You can choose from two types of photo printers — inkjet and dye sublimation. Photo printers are designed to print photos well, but may not print text documents as well. Multipurpose printers print text documents well, but typically do not print high-quality photos. Both inkjet and dye sublimation printers produce high-quality prints, with some people preferring the output qualities of one type over the other.

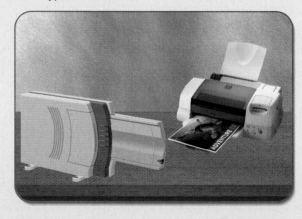

Inkjet Printers

Inkjet printers spray fine droplets of ink from one to seven ink cartridges. With some, you can print enlargements of 11 by 14 inches and larger. Look for printers with light-fast and fade-resistant inks and papers. Some manufacturers guarantee colorfastness only if you use their premium papers and inks. Inkjet printers range in price from less than $100 up to $700.

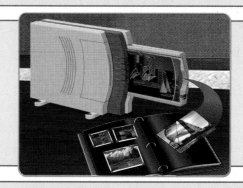

Dye Sublimation Printers

Dye sublimation printers create very high-quality, continuous-tone prints that resemble traditional photo prints. You can print up to 8" x 10"-inch prints only using ribbons and paper designed for dye sublimation printing. Some dye sublimation printers print a UV coating on the prints to increase colorfastness. Dye sublimation printers range in price from $100 to $1,000.

Resolution

Printer resolution refers to how the printer places ink on the page and the number of dots it prints per inch. Generally the higher the number of dots, the finer the tonal subtleties in the print. Some printers use lower resolutions but layer dots to create fine tonality in prints. Resolutions range from 2880 dpi to 720. However, higher resolutions consume more ink, and require more printing time.

Printer Speed

An advertised print speed usually refers to speed for printing text or low-quality photo prints. Few printers produce an 8" x 10"-inch print in less than five minutes at high-quality settings, such as 1440 dpi.

Print Quality

Just as you would not buy a car without driving it, you should evaluate print samples from different printers before you purchase one. When you evaluate the sample prints, look for continuous color that is not streaking, or banding, color that is vivid but realistic, and good reproduction of fine detail and of dark, light, and midtones.

MATCHING PRINTS TO SCREEN DISPLAY

Matching what you see on the screen to what you see in a photo print can be a challenge. To match color, you can use a simple, no-cost technique, or a sophisticated, expensive technique that creates device profiles.

What to Expect

Most people expect printed photos to reproduce the vivid colors they see on the monitor. However, a monitor displays more colors than a printer can reproduce. You can have a better color match when you create color profiles that accurately describe the color gamut — the range of colors that your monitor and your printer share.

Basic Color Management

Professional photographers use color management to ensure accurate color. This means they use the same color space, or range of colors, from editing through printing to ensure reliable results. You can start basic color management, by choosing the Adobe color space in Photoshop Elements and by calibrating your monitor as described in Chapter 10.

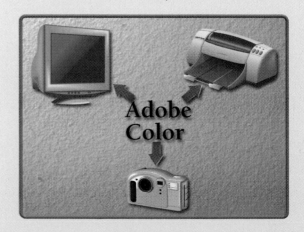

Match Color the No-Cost Way

If colors in photo prints differ from colors you see on the screen, then you can adjust image color using your image-editing program or the printer color settings. If colors are too warm, then edit the image to decrease the red hue. As an alternative, you can adjust printer color settings, described later in this chapter.

Use a Color Calibration System

You can buy color calibration hardware and software that measures device color to help ensure consistent results for your monitor and printer. Devices measure monitor color and create color profiles that describe the color range of the device. You can choose from a variety of devices ranging in price from $300 to $1,000.

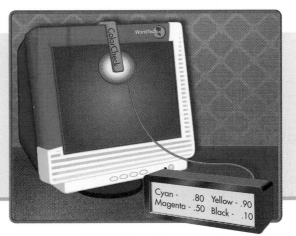

Keep Camera Settings Consistent

If you print photos at home, then you can help ensure consistent color by using the techniques provided in this book, and by keeping your camera settings consistent. If you frequently set the camera options to bump up the color, saturation, or contrast, then your print results can vary accordingly. Find settings that produce good images, and then use them consistently.

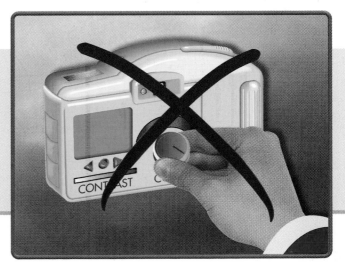

ADD A PICTURE CAPTION

Before printing your picture, you can add text as a caption that prints with the picture.

Jack's First Game

ADD A PICTURE CAPTION

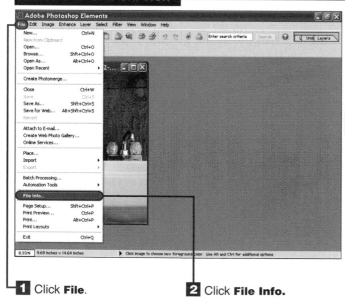

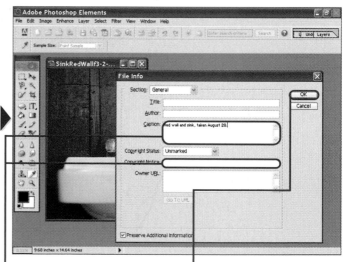

1 Click **File**.

2 Click **File Info.**

■ The File Info dialog box appears.

3 Click inside the Caption box and type the caption text you want.

■ You can type copyright information to display a copyright line in the window title bar.

4 Click **OK.**

*Note: Caption text appears when you print the photo and select **Caption** in the Print Preview dialog box.*

After you edit your picture, you can send it to an online service like Shutterfly or MSN photos for online printing from within Photoshop Elements. Your image file uploads to the online service, and then you can select the size print you want or the photo gift item you want. Prints are delivered to you via mail.

PRINT TO AN ONLINE SERVICE

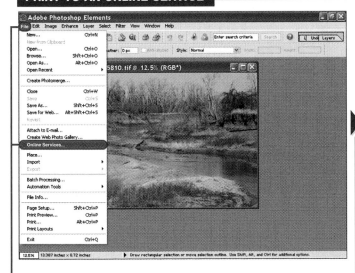

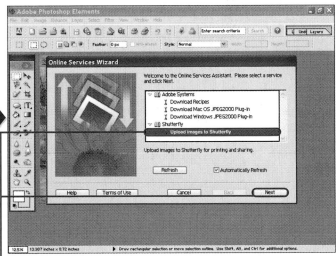

1 Click **File**.

2 Click **Online Services.**

■ Photoshop Elements downloads a list of service providers.

■ The Online Services Wizard dialog box appears.

3 Click a service.

4 Click **Next.**

5 Click **OK.**

6 Follow the directions on the screen to complete the upload.

■ Photoshop Elements uploads photos for printing.

OPTIMIZE PRINTER SETTINGS

Like cameras, printers can display color characteristics unique to the printer or printer brand. You can adjust printer driver settings to fine-tune color. You can also set standard print settings using this technique.

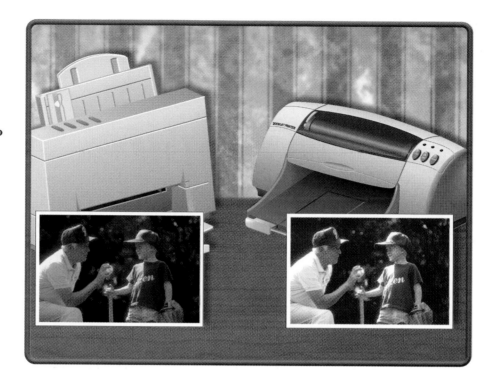

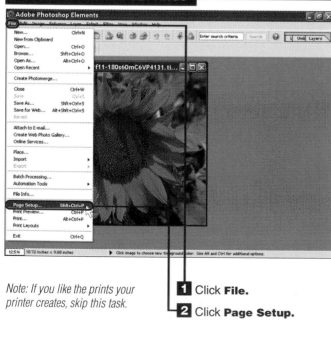

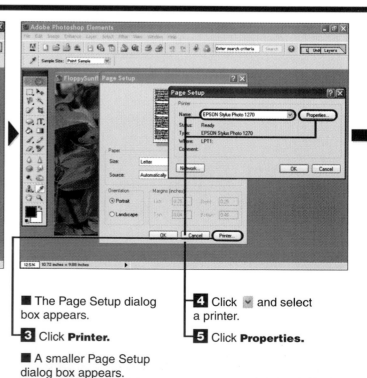

Note: If you like the prints your printer creates, skip this task.

1 Click **File**.

2 Click **Page Setup**.

■ The Page Setup dialog box appears.

3 Click **Printer**.

■ A smaller Page Setup dialog box appears.

4 Click ☑ and select a printer.

5 Click **Properties**.

What should I know about default printer driver settings?

Most printer drivers set the print resolution to low or medium. For the best results, select the highest-quality setting. If your printer offers a photo enhance option, then try printing a test picture with the option turned on, and then with the option turned off. Evaluate the pictures to see which produces the best print.

How do I prevent banding in my prints?

You can often prevent banding, or the appearance of wide streaks across prints, by cleaning the printer heads. Most printers come with a utility that allows you to clean and align printer heads periodically. Check the printer manual for details.

■ The properties dialog box for your printer appears.

■ Depending on the printer, you can select the paper type, speed, print resolution, and other options.

6 Select the options you want.

■ For best results, always select the paper type and size that matches the paper you use.

■ You can click other tabs in the printer properties dialog box that apply and select the options you want.

■ Photoshop Elements applies the page setup options.

CREATE A CONTACT SHEET

You can print a
contact sheet that
shows thumbnail-size
versions of all the
pictures in a folder.
You can use the
contact sheet to
evaluate pictures
you want to edit.

CREATE A CONTACT SHEET

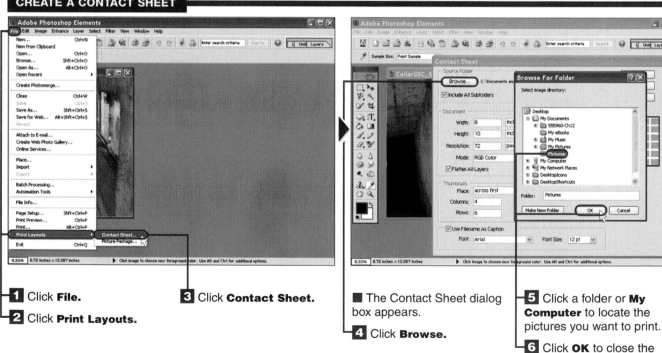

1 Click **File**.

2 Click **Print Layouts**.

3 Click **Contact Sheet**.

■ The Contact Sheet dialog
box appears.

4 Click **Browse**.

5 Click a folder or **My
Computer** to locate the
pictures you want to print.

6 Click **OK** to close the
Browse For Folder
dialog box.

What should I do with old contact sheets?

You can use old contact sheets as a visual index for folders of pictures you burn to a recordable CD or DVD. You can tape the contact sheet to the jewel case for quick reference. You can also use the filename as a caption on the contact sheet if you check the option in the Contact Sheet dialog box.

Why should I print contact sheets at high resolution?

Printing a contact sheet at the default 72 dpi resolution produces a very low-quality version of the pictures, making it difficult to judge photo quality. If you want to save ink, then you can print contact sheets at 150 or 240 dpi instead of the full 300 dpi resolution.

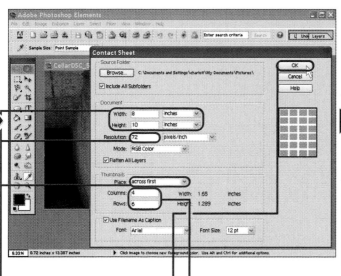

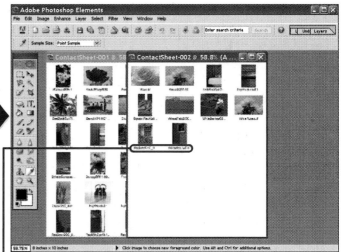

7 Type the paper dimensions.

■ Click ❤ to change the unit of measure.

8 Type a resolution.

■ Typing **240** or **300** creates a high-quality contact sheet.

9 Click ❤ and select the order for image placement.

10 Type values for the number of columns and rows.

■ Printing fewer columns results in larger thumbnails on the contact sheet.

11 Click **OK.**

■ Photoshop Elements builds the contact sheet and displays a preview.

■ Filenames appear below each thumbnail.

■ If the folder contains many photos, then Photoshop Elements creates multiple contact sheets and numbers them.

Before printing, you can preview how the image fits on the page and modify printer settings. Use Print Preview to help avoid wasting photo paper.

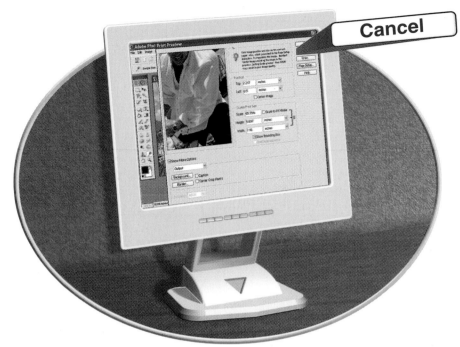

Cancel

PREVIEW AND PRINT A PHOTO

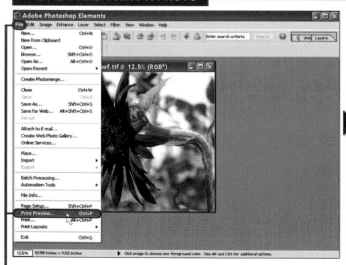

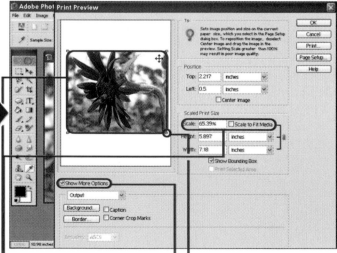

■1 Click **File**.

■2 Click **Print Preview**.

■ The Print Preview dialog box appears.

■ If the image is larger than the page, then type a smaller percentage, or click **Scale to Fit Media**.

■ You can click and drag the bounding box to resize the picture for the page.

■ Clicking a corner handle on the bounding box proportionally resizes the photo on the page

■3 Click **Show More Options** (☐ changes to ☑).

Can I use color management for printing?

You can choose color management options in Photoshop Elements.

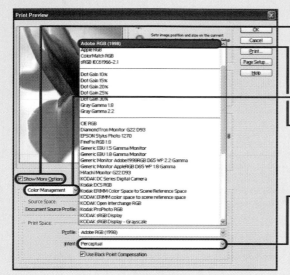

1 In the Print Preview dialog box, click
Show More Options (☐ changes to ☑).

■ Photoshop Elements displays more print options.

2 Click ▾ and select **Color Management**.

3 Click ▾ and select the profile for your printer.

■ If your printer profile does not appear in the list, then you can download it from the manufacturer's Web site.

4 Click ▾ and select **Perceptual**.

■ The Perceptual option preserves a natural appearance of photo colors. For business presentations, select **Saturation**.

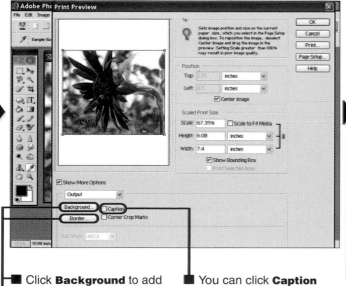

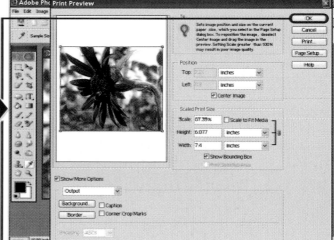

■ Click **Background** to add a background color behind the photo.

■ Click **Border** and then type a value for the border width in the Border dialog box.

■ You can click **Caption** (☐ changes to ☑) to include a caption you typed in the file information dialog box.

Note: See the section "Add a Picture Caption" to enter caption text.

4 Click **OK**

■ Photoshop Elements prints the photo.

PRINT A PICTURE PACKAGE

To share your best prints with family and friends, you can print various sizes of one or more pictures on a single page using the Photoshop Elements Picture Package.

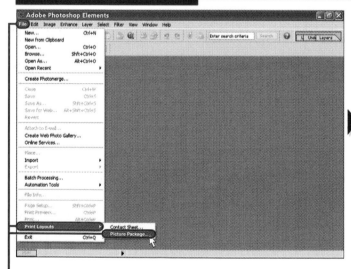

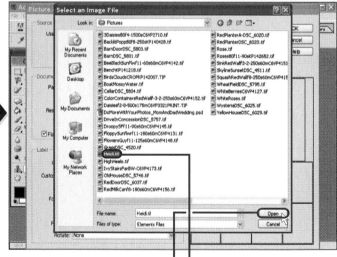

1 Click **File**.

2 Click **Print Layouts**.

3 Click **Picture Package**.

■ The Picture Package dialog box appears. If you have a picture open, Photoshop Elements displays it in the default package layout.

4 Click **Browse** to change pictures.

■ The Select an Image File dialog box appears.

5 Click the file or folder you want.

6 Click **Open**.

What is the best way to set up a Picture Package with multiple photos?

If you want to put multiple photos in the Picture Package, then you can create a folder that contains only the pictures you want first. Pictures you include should be edited, sharpened, and ready to print. Then you can select the folder you created in the Picture Package dialog box.

What if my pictures have text layers?

In the Picture Package dialog box, you can click **Flatten All Layers** (☐ changes to ☑) to flatten the layers so that text prints on the picture.

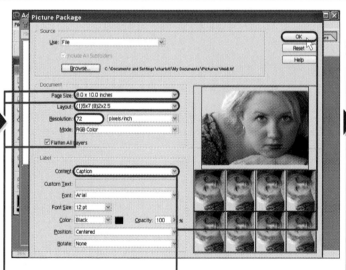

■ The picture or pictures you chose appear in the Picture Package dialog box.

7 Click ⌄ and select a page size.

8 Click ⌄ and select the layout.

9 Type in a resolution.

■ For best results, type **240** or **300**.

■ You can click ⌄ to include caption text.

Note: See "Create a Picture Caption" earlier in this chapter.

10 Click **OK.**

■ Photoshop Elements sizes and displays the picture package.

11 To print the package, click the Print button (🖨).

Note: For more information on printing a photo, see "Preview and Print a Photo."

My Vacation Pictures

CHAPTER 14

Share Photos Electronically

You can display digital photos on your computer and share them electronically with family and friends. This chapter shows you creative ways to use your digital photos.

You can personalize your computer monitor or LCD by displaying one or more of your digital photos as a desktop background.

DISPLAY A PHOTO ON YOUR DESKTOP

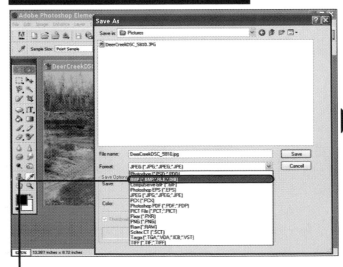

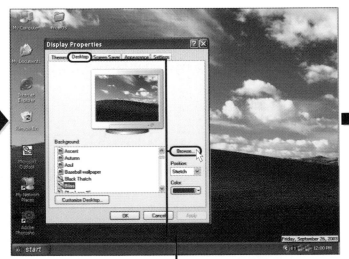

1 Open a picture and save it in BMP format.

■ When Photoshop Elements asks you to confirm the Window format, click **OK.**

Note: See Chapter 10 for instructions on saving a file.

2 Right-click an empty area on the desktop.

3 Click **Properties.**

■ The Display Properties dialog box appears.

4 Click the **Desktop** tab.

5 Click **Browse.**

Can I customize the look of my desktop to match the picture?

In Windows XP, you can change the color scheme and background colors of your desktop by selecting options on the Desktop tab in the Display Properties dialog box. (In older versions of Windows, click the **Appearance** tab.) Then, click **Colors** and then **More** to see additional colors.

How can I improve the fit of my picture on the screen?

Because monitors and LCDs are wider than they are tall, horizontal pictures fit better on a screen than vertical pictures. If you want a vertical picture, then try selecting **Tile** in the Position box, or select **Center**, and then select a coordinating color in the Color box.

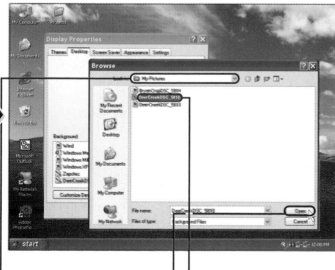

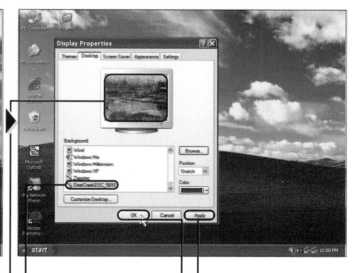

■ The Browse dialog box appears.

6 Navigate to the folder containing the picture you want.

7 Click the file.

8 Click **Open**.

■ Windows adds the file to the Background list.

9 Click the filename of the picture you want.

■ The image appears in the preview area.

■ To make your photo fit the screen, select Stretch.

10 Click **Apply**.

■ Your photo appears on the desktop.

11 Click **OK**.

CREATE A SLIDESHOW SCREEN SAVER

For fun, you can create a slideshow of your favorite photos. The slideshow runs when the computer is inactive for the amount of time you specify. You can set the size of the pictures, timing, and add transition effects for the slideshow.

CREATE A SLIDESHOW SCREEN SAVER

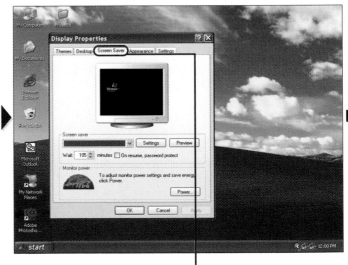

1 On your computer desktop, right-click in an empty area.

2 Click **Properties.**

■ The Display Properties dialog box appears.

3 Click the **Screen Saver** tab.

How can I change the pictures in the screen saver?

The slideshow displays pictures in the My Pictures folder, located in the My Documents folder on the desktop by default. You can add the pictures you want for the slideshow to that folder, or you can change folders. In the Display Properties dialog box, click **Settings** on the Screen Saver tab and then click **Browse** to choose a different folder.

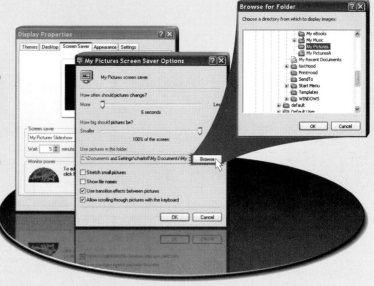

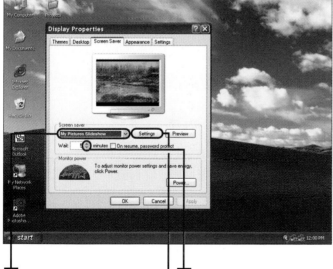

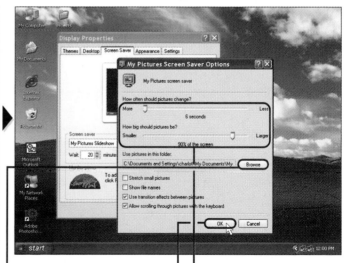

4 Click ⌄ and select **My Pictures Slideshow.**

5 Click ⬍ to select the wait time before the slideshow screen saver begins.

6 Click **Settings.**

■ The My Pictures Screen Saver Options dialog box appears.

7 Click **Browse** and select the folder containing the images you want.

8 Click **OK.**

9 Set the timing and size of the pictures.

10 Click **OK** to close the Display Properties dialog box.

■ The screen saver displays after the computer is inactive for the specified wait time.

SHARE PHOTOS THROUGH E-MAIL

You can send photos in an e-mail message to keep friends and family up-to-date on events, and children as they grow.

SHARE PHOTOS THROUGH E-MAIL

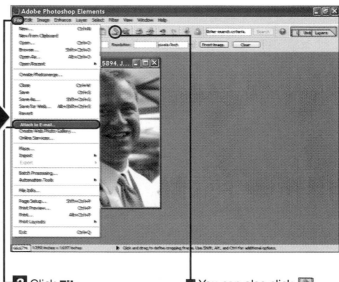

1 Open the image you want to attach to an e-mail message.

Note: See Chapter 10 to open an image.

2 Click **File**.

3 Click **Attach to E-mail.**

■ You can also click .

Why should I use JPEG format for e-mailing pictures?

JPEG format compresses images to a smaller file size. Some e-mail systems set limits on the size of e-mail attachments that you can send. If you send a picture in TIFF format, then the file size will likely be too large for the recipient to receive. When you send a low-resolution JPEG, the recipient can quickly and easily open and view the smaller image file.

Can I send a picture so it appears within the text of a message?

Yes. First, save a JPEG copy of the picture at a low-resolution setting. Then set your e-mail format to HTML. Some e-mail programs may not offer HTML format. Create a new e-mail message, click **Insert,** then click **Picture**, and then browse to the folder that contains the picture. Choose the options you want, and click **OK** to display the picture in the e-mail message.

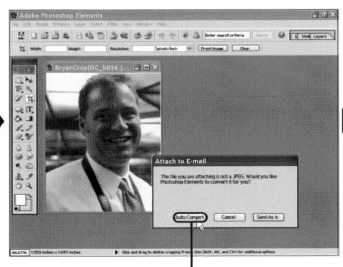

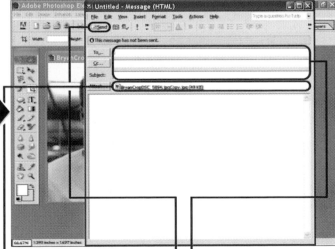

■ If the image is not in JPEG format, then the Attach to E-mail dialog box appears.

4 Click **Auto Convert.**

■ Photoshop Elements converts the picture to JPEG format.

■ Photoshop Elements starts your default e-mail program, and creates a new message with the picture attached.

5 Type the e-mail address of the recipient, a subject, and the text of the message.

6 Click **Send.**

CREATE A WEB PHOTO GALLERY

Displaying pictures on a Web site usually requires hours of work. However, you can use Photoshop Elements to automatically create the layout and to size photos for a professional-looking, online photo gallery.

CREATE A WEB PHOTO GALLERY

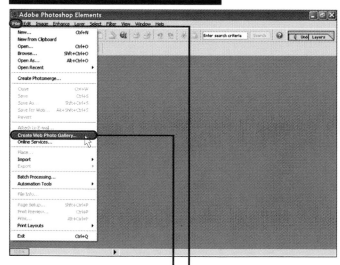

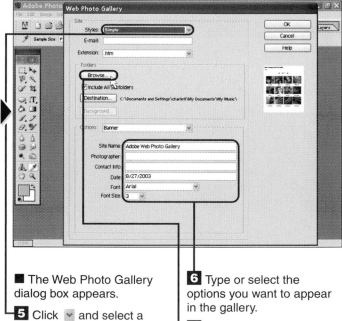

1 Create a folder on your computer for your gallery pictures.

2 Copy or move gallery pictures to the new folder.

3 Click **File**.

4 Click **Create Web Photo Gallery**.

■ The Web Photo Gallery dialog box appears.

5 Click ✔ and select a gallery style.

6 Type or select the options you want to appear in the gallery.

7 Click **Browse**.

What if my Web site does not use frames?

If you do not use frames on your Web site, then you can select one of the simple gallery styles, such as Simple or Table. You can modify the code that Photoshop Elements creates in an HTML editor, such as Microsoft FrontPage.

How do I incorporate the gallery on my Web site?

You can copy all of the files that Elements creates to a folder on your site. You can use the index.htm page as your home page or as a subpage. You can rename the file that Photoshop Elements creates if index.htm is the name of your current home page. You can modify the photo order by editing the index.htm file.

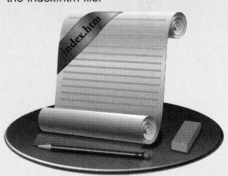

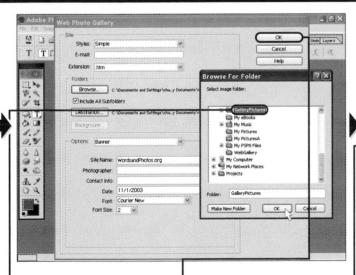

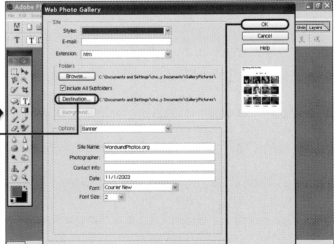

■ The Browse For dialog box appears.

8 Click the folder containing the gallery images.

9 Click **OK** to close the Browse for Folder dialog box.

10 Click **Destination**, and repeat steps **8** and **9** to select a folder to which you want to save the finished gallery.

11 Click **OK**.

CONTINUED

CREATE A WEB PHOTO GALLERY

With very little work, you can share special occasion photos with family and friends by creating new Web photo galleries for each special occasion.

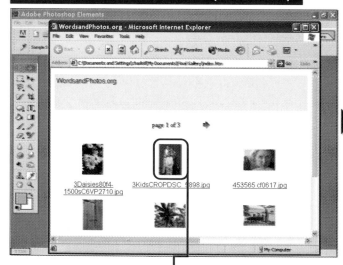

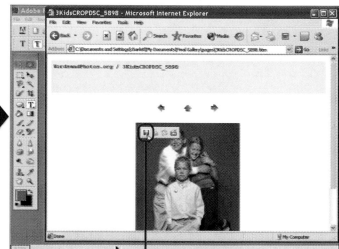

■ Photoshop Elements opens images, sizes them, creates thumbnails, and creates the gallery HTML code.

■ Photoshop Elements displays the gallery in the default Web browser window.

■ You can click a thumbnail to see a larger version of the image.

■ The full-size version of the photo appears in your browser window.

■ People visiting your Web photo gallery can save a copy of your photo by clicking the photo, and then clicking the Windows picture bar and choosing Save This Picture.

UPLOAD PHOTOS TO A PHOTO-SHARING WEB SITE

You can share photos
with friends, family, and
other photo enthusiasts
by uploading images to a
photo-sharing Web site.
Most sites offer photo-
printing services as well
as photo sharing.

UPLOAD PHOTOS TO A PHOTO-SHARING WEB SITE

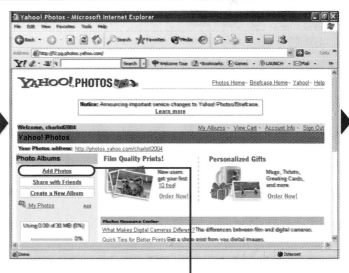

*Note: Steps for uploading photos
vary by site. The following steps
apply to Yahoo!.*

■ Sign up for, and sign into,
your photo-sharing site.

1 Click **Photos.**

■ The Yahoo! Photos page
appears.

2 Click **Add Photos.**

CONTINUED

UPLOAD PHOTOS TO A PHOTO-SHARING WEB SITE

When you upload high-resolution photos to many popular Web photo-sharing sites, you can give your family and friends permission to order prints from your images. For example, grandparents can easily print recent pictures of the grandchildren that you post on a site.

Say hello to your first grandchild, Mark Allen. This adorable little angel weighs 7lbs., 2oz., and has his mother's red hair.

UPLOAD PHOTOS TO A PHOTO-SHARING WEB SITE (CONTINUED)

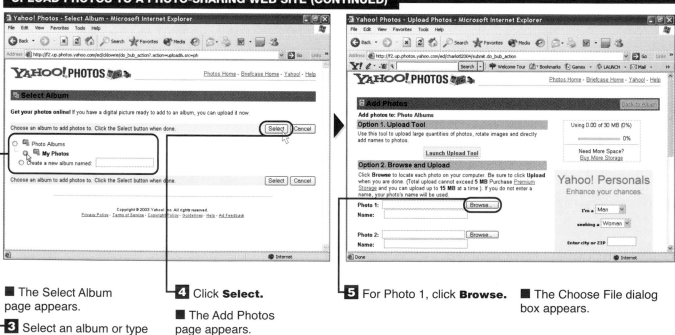

■ The Select Album page appears.

3 Select an album or type a name for a new album.

4 Click **Select.**

■ The Add Photos page appears.

5 For Photo 1, click **Browse.**

■ The Choose File dialog box appears.

Should I upload low-resolution or high-resolution photos?

If you want to only show pictures to friends, you can upload low-resolution photos. If you want to make prints, enlargements, or photo novelty items, such as a calendar or t-shirt, then you should upload high-resolution pictures. Most sites allow you to limit who can view and access your photos. Check the resolution guidelines on the site for specific requirements and limitations.

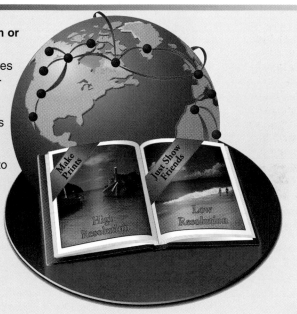

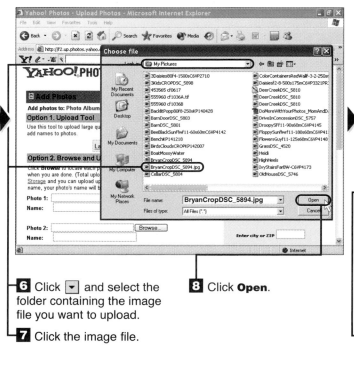

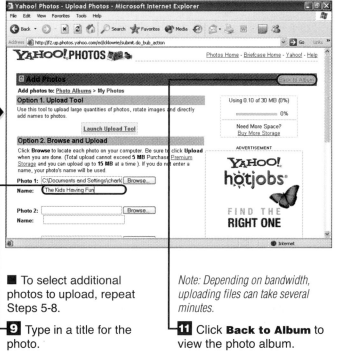

6 Click ▾ and select the folder containing the image file you want to upload.

7 Click the image file.

8 Click **Open**.

■ To select additional photos to upload, repeat Steps 5-8.

9 Type in a title for the photo.

10 Click **Upload**.

Note: Depending on bandwidth, uploading files can take several minutes.

11 Click **Back to Album** to view the photo album.

257

PREVIEW AN IMAGE IN A BROWSER

If you plan on using
your edited images on
the Web, you can see
how your image looks
in a browser window.
You can find the
option for previewing
in a browser in the
Save For Web dialog
box. You can choose
from any of the Web
browser applications
installed on your
computer or launch
your default browser
to preview the image.

PREVIEW AN IMAGE IN A BROWSER

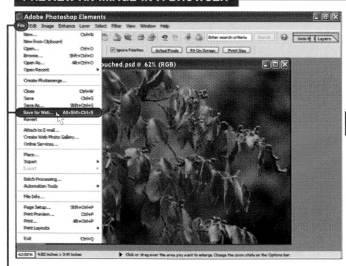

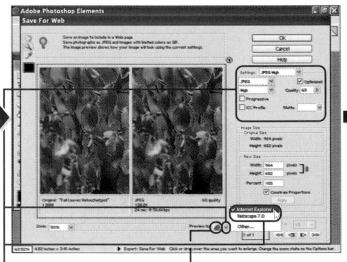

1 Click **File**.

2 Click **Save for Web**.

■ You can also click the
Save for Web button (🖼)
on the Shortcuts bar.

■ The Save For Web dialog
box appears.

3 Select any optimizing
options you want to apply.

4 Click the Preview In ▾.

5 Click a browser.

■ You can also click the
Internet Explorer browser
icon (🖼) to open Internet
Explorer.

■ If you have more than
one browser installed, click
Other and navigate to the
browser you want to open.

How do I add a browser to the Preview menu in the Save For Web dialog box?

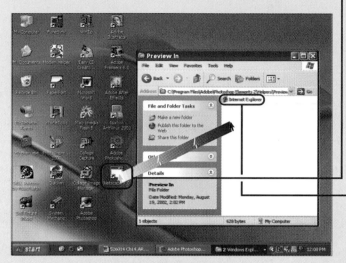

1 Create a shortcut icon for the browser on your desktop.

2 Using your computer's folder navigation window, click the Photoshop Elements program folder.

3 Click the Helpers folder.

4 Double-click the Preview In folder.

Note: See your program's documentation to create a shortcut and to navigate to folders.

5 Click and drag the browser icon and place it in the Preview In folder.

■ The next time you open Elements and use the Save For Web dialog box, the browser is added to the available selections.

■ The browser launches and displays the image.

■ This example shows an image in Microsoft Internet Explorer.

6 Click ⊠ (●).

7 Click **OK**.

■ Elements continues saving the file for the Web.

■ You can click **Cancel** to exit the dialog box without saving your changes.

MAKE A PDF SLIDESHOW

Elements can save several images as a single PDF file that can play as a slideshow. You can set how often the slides change and whether the slideshow repeats.

PDF stands for Portable Document Format, a file format developed by Adobe. You can open PDF files with Adobe Acrobat, which you can download for free at www.adobe.com/acrobat/.

MAKE A PDF SLIDESHOW

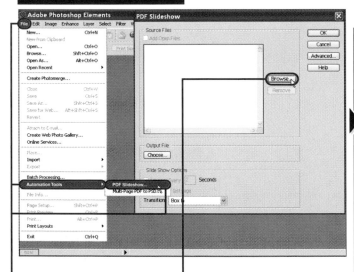

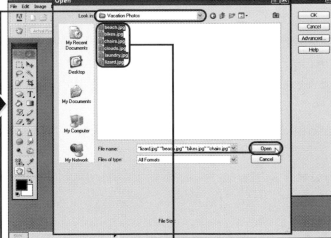

1 Click **File**.

2 Click **Automation Tools**.

3 Click **PDF Slideshow**.

■ The PDF Slideshow dialog box appears.

4 Click **Browse**.

5 Click ☑ and drag the scroll bar to select the folder that contains the images you want to use.

6 Press **Shift** and click to select the images.

7 Click **Open**.

What are slideshow transitions?

Transitions are the effects that occur as one slide in the slideshow replaces another. You can click and specify one of 18 different transitions in the Transition box located in the PDF Slideshow dialog box. For example, you can make your slides appear in stripes like window blinds with the **Blinds** transitions. With the **Glitter** transitions, new slides appear as randomly scattered squares. **Wipe** transitions bring new slides in from one of the four sides of the screen.

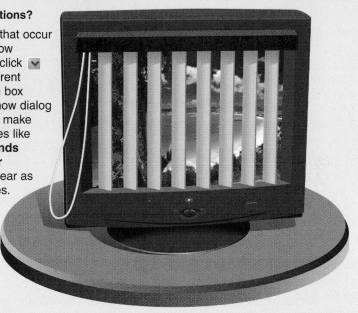

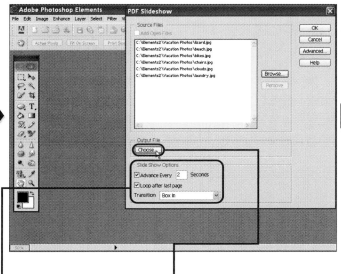

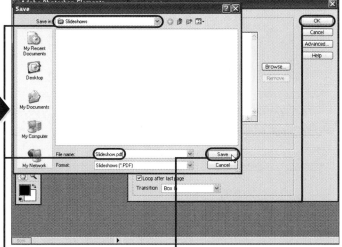

■ Elements lists the files in the Source Files list.

8 Click (☐ changes to ☑) or type values to specify your slideshow options.

■ You can specify how fast the slideshow moves, whether it loops (repeats), and the transition effects that appear between the slides.

9 Click **Choose**.

■ The Save dialog box appears.

10 Click and select the folder in which to save the slideshow.

11 Type a name for the slideshow.

Note: PDF filenames must end in .pdf.

12 Click **Save**.

13 Click **OK** in the PDF Slideshow dialog box.

■ Elements saves the slideshow.

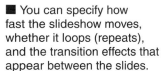

CHAPTER 15

Create Print Projects

You can take, edit, and print digital photos, and you can also use finished photos to create fun and useful projects, and to help with everyday tasks. This chapter shows some of the possibilities.

DO MORE WITH YOUR PHOTOS

Whether you print your own photo projects or have a commercial service print them, you can use photos for a variety of projects and everyday tasks.

For detailed information on the tasks mentioned here, consult your software documentation or customer support.

Create Photo Gifts and Projects

Photo sites, such as MSN Photos, Yahoo!, Ofoto, and Shutterfly, offer a variety of photo projects that range from photo puzzles to photo books, cards, and postcards.

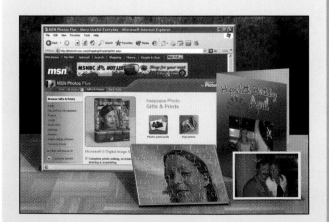

Using Online Services

The process for creating print projects using online services is very similar to that described in Chapter 14. If you upload high-resolution photos, then you can create high-quality and custom photo postcards, t-shirts, and other novelty items.

Do-It-Yourself Photo Projects

Many programs, such as Microsoft® Digital Image Pro, include project templates that you can use to create calendars, brochures, presentations, and stationery that include space for photos. You can buy specialty photo papers in different textures and weights to give projects a professional look.

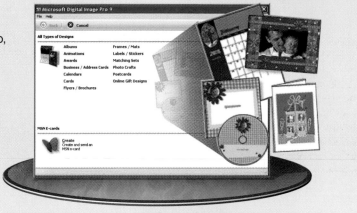

Add Variety to Business Projects

Consider using digital photos in business projects — including newsletters, presentations, and brochures — in instructional documentation and on Web sites.

Make Everyday Tasks Easier

You can use your digital camera for everyday tasks, including showing previous projects in your resume, for comparison-shopping, to describe objects or projects to others, and to document damage to property. If you sell items through online auction sites, then you can use your digital camera to show the items you are selling.

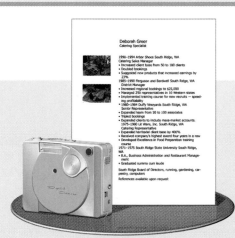

CREATE A PHOTO CALENDAR IN WORD

You can create and print calendars that feature your original photos. Programs such as Microsoft Digital Image Pro, Word, and Publisher include templates to create a variety of print photo projects.

This task requires the Calendar template included with the full installation option of Word. To install this template, refer to your Microsoft Word documentation.

CREATE A PHOTO CALENDAR IN WORD

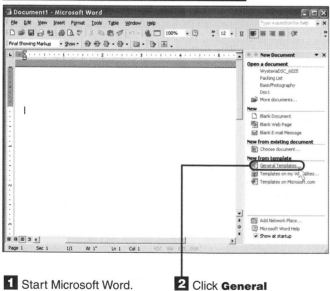

1 Start Microsoft Word.

2 Click **General Templates.**

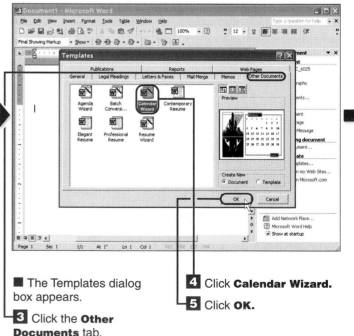

■ The Templates dialog box appears.

3 Click the **Other Documents** tab.

4 Click **Calendar Wizard.**

5 Click **OK.**

How can I insert my own picture in the calendar?

You can replace the default picture with your own picture using this technique.

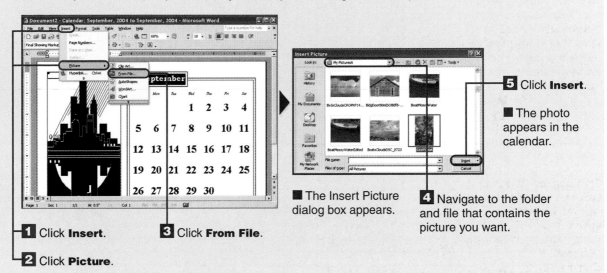

1 Click **Insert**.

2 Click **Picture**.

3 Click **From File**.

■ The Insert Picture dialog box appears.

4 Navigate to the folder and file that contains the picture you want.

5 Click **Insert**.

■ The photo appears in the calendar.

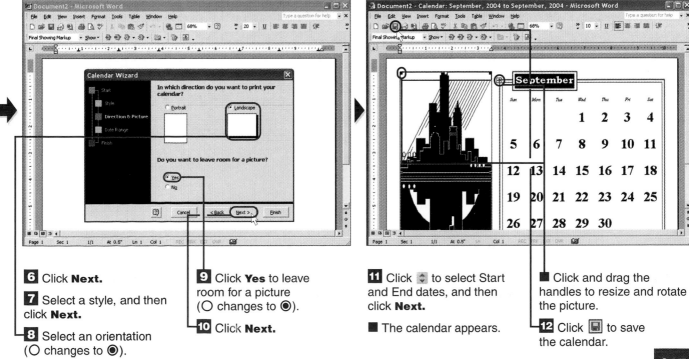

6 Click **Next**.

7 Select a style, and then click **Next**.

8 Select an orientation (○ changes to ◉).

9 Click **Yes** to leave room for a picture (○ changes to ◉).

10 Click **Next**.

11 Click ☐ to select Start and End dates, and then click **Next**.

■ The calendar appears.

■ Click and drag the handles to resize and rotate the picture.

12 Click ☐ to save the calendar.

CREATE A HOME INVENTORY USING EXCEL

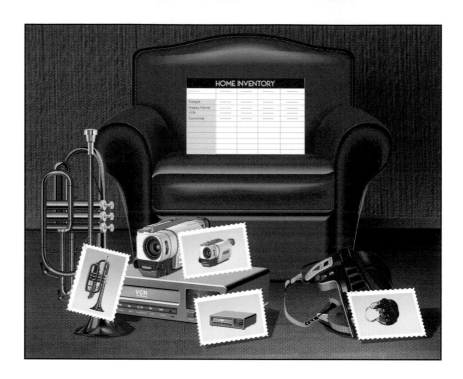

You can compile a home inventory that includes pictures of all or some of your home possessions. Be sure to keep the inventory up-to-date and provide a copy to your insurance company.

CREATE A HOME INVENTORY USING EXCEL

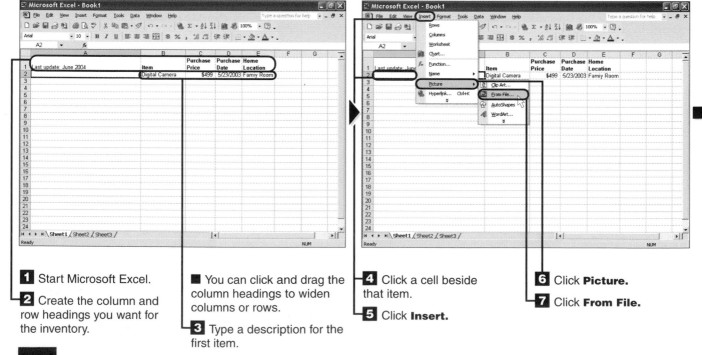

1 Start Microsoft Excel.

2 Create the column and row headings you want for the inventory.

■ You can click and drag the column headings to widen columns or rows.

3 Type a description for the first item.

4 Click a cell beside that item.

5 Click **Insert**.

6 Click **Picture**.

7 Click **From File**.

Do I need to size pictures before inserting them into the inventory?

No. You can change the size of the pictures within Excel to either 96 dpi for screen display or 200 dpi for printing using the **Compress Picture** button, on the Picture toolbar in Excel, to reduce the size. However, it is a good idea to create JPEG versions of the pictures before you insert them into the spreadsheet.

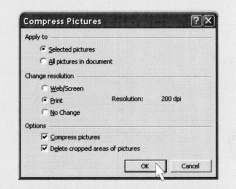

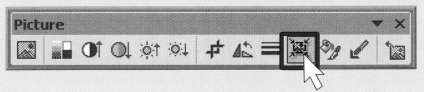

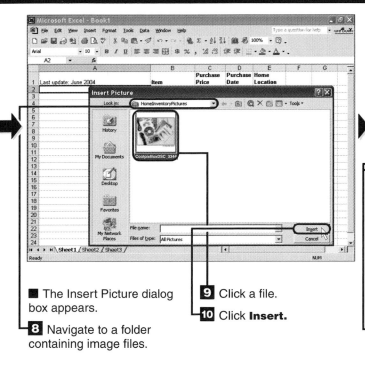

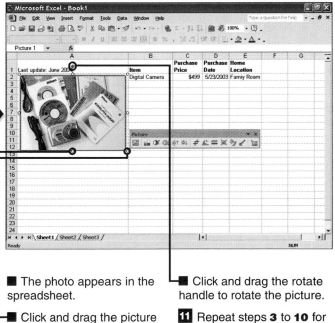

■ The Insert Picture dialog box appears.

8 Navigate to a folder containing image files.

9 Click a file.

10 Click **Insert.**

■ The photo appears in the spreadsheet.

■ Click and drag the picture handles to resize the picture.

■ Click and drag the rotate handle to rotate the picture.

11 Repeat steps **3** to **10** for each item in the inventory.

Introducing Our New Consumer Books...

Our new Teach Yourself VISUALLY Consumer books are an excellent resource for people who want to learn more about general interest topics. We have launched this new groundbreaking series with three exciting titles: *Teach Yourself VISUALLY Weight Training, Teach Yourself VISUALLY Yoga,* and *Teach Yourself VISUALLY Guitar*. These books maintain the same design and structure of our computer books— graphical, two-page lessons that are jam-packed with useful, easy-to-understand information.

Each full-color book includes over **500** photographs, accompanied by step-by-step instructions to guide you through the fundamentals of each topic. "Teach Yourself" sidebars also provide practical tips and tricks to further fine tune your skills and introduce more advanced techniques.

By using top experts in their respective fields to consult on our books, we offer our readers an extraordinary opportunity to access first-class, superior knowledge in conjunction with our award winning communication process. Teach Yourself VISUALLY Consumer is simply the best way to learn!

Teach Yourself VISUALLY **WEIGHT TRAINING**

ISBN: 0-7645-2582-4
Price: $24.99 US; $36.99 CDN; £14.99 UK
Page count: 320

Teach Yourself VISUALLY **YOGA**

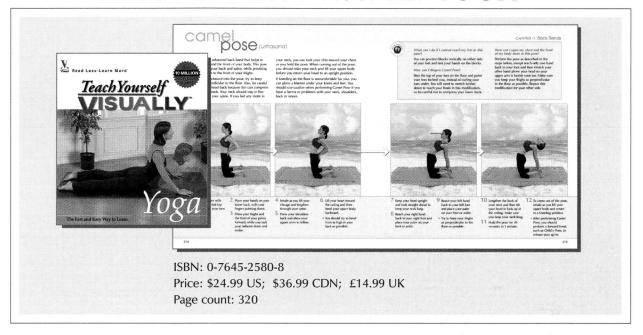

ISBN: 0-7645-2580-8
Price: $24.99 US; $36.99 CDN; £14.99 UK
Page count: 320

Teach Yourself VISUALLY **GUITAR**

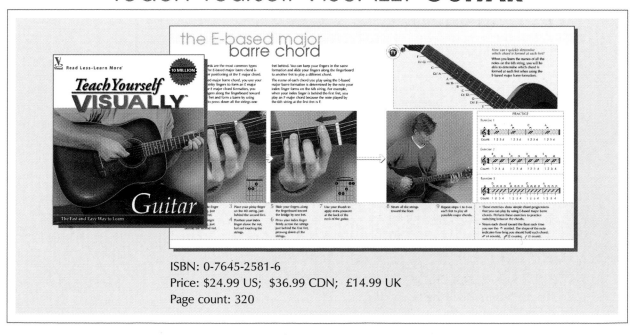

ISBN: 0-7645-2581-6
Price: $24.99 US; $36.99 CDN; £14.99 UK
Page count: 320

Read Less – Learn More®

Visual

Simplified®

Simply the Easiest Way to Learn

For visual learners who are brand-new to a topic and want to be shown, not told, how to solve a problem in a friendly, approachable way.

All *Simplified®* books feature friendly Disk characters who demonstrate and explain the purpose of each task.

Title	ISBN	Price
America Online Simplified, 2nd Ed.	0-7645-3433-5	$27.99
America Online Simplified, 3rd Ed.	0-7645-3673-7	$24.99
Computers Simplified, 5th Ed.	0-7645-3524-2	$27.99
Creating Web Pages with HTML Simplified, 2nd Ed.	0-7645-6067-0	$27.99
Excel 2002 Simplified	0-7645-3589-7	$27.99
FrontPage 2000 Simplified	0-7645-3450-5	$27.99
FrontPage 2002 Simplified	0-7645-3612-5	$27.99
Internet and World Wide Web Simplified, 3rd Ed.	0-7645-3409-2	$27.99
Microsoft Excel 2000 Simplified	0-7645-6053-0	$27.99
Microsoft Office 2000 Simplified	0-7645-6052-2	$29.99
Microsoft Word 2000 Simplified	0-7645-6054-9	$27.99
More Windows 98 Simplified	0-7645-6037-9	$27.99
Office XP Simplified	0-7645-0850-4	$29.99
PC Upgrade and Repair Simplified, 2nd Ed.	0-7645-3560-9	$27.99
Windows 98 Simplified	0-7645-6030-1	$27.99
Windows Me Millennium Edition Simplified	0-7645-3494-7	$27.99
Windows XP Simplified	0-7645-3618-4	$27.99
Word 2002 Simplified	0-7645-3588-9	$27.99

with these full-color Visual™ guides

The Fast and Easy Way to Learn

Discover how to use what you learn with "Teach Yourself" tips

Title	ISBN	Price
Teach Yourself FrontPage 2000 VISUALLY	0-7645-3451-3	$29.99
Teach Yourself HTML VISUALLY	0-7645-3423-8	$29.99
Teach Yourself the Internet and World Wide Web VISUALLY, 2nd Ed.	0-7645-3410-6	$29.99
Teach Yourself Microsoft Access 2000 VISUALLY	0-7645-6059-X	$29.99
Teach Yourself Microsoft Excel 2000 VISUALLY	0-7645-6056-5	$29.99
Teach Yourself Microsoft Office 2000 VISUALLY	0-7645-6051-4	$29.99
Teach Yourself VISUALLY Access 2002	0-7645-3691-9	$29.99
Teach Yourself VISUALLY Adobe Acrobat 5 PDF	0-7645-3667-2	$29.99
Teach Yourself VISUALLY Adobe Premiere 6	0-7645-3664-8	$29.99
Teach Yourself VISUALLY Computers, 3rd Ed.	0-7645-3525-0	$29.99
Teach Yourself VISUALLY Digital Photography	0-7645-3565-X	$29.99
Teach Yourself VISUALLY Digital Video	0-7645-3688-5	$29.99
Teach Yourself VISUALLY Dreamweaver MX	0-7645-3694-7	$29.99
Teach Yourself VISUALLY E-commerce with FrontPage	0-7645-3579-X	$29.99
Teach Yourself VISUALLY Excel 2002	0-7645-3594-3	$29.99
Teach Yourself VISUALLY Fireworks 4	0-7645-3566-8	$29.99
Teach Yourself VISUALLY Flash MX	0-7645-3661-3	$29.99
Teach Yourself VISUALLY Flash 5	0-7645-3540-4	$29.99
Teach Yourself VISUALLY FrontPage 2002	0-7645-3590-0	$29.99
Teach Yourself VISUALLY Illustrator 10	0-7645-3654-0	$29.99
Teach Yourself VISUALLY iMac	0-7645-3453-X	$29.99
Teach Yourself VISUALLY Investing Online	0-7645-3459-9	$29.99
Teach Yourself VISUALLY Mac OS X v. 10.2 Jaguar	0-7645-1802-X	$29.99
Teach Yourself VISUALLY Macromedia Web Collection	0-7645-3648-6	$39.99
Teach Yourself VISUALLY More Windows XP	0-7645-3698-2	$29.99
Teach Yourself VISUALLY Networking, 2nd Ed.	0-7645-3534-X	$29.99
Teach Yourself VISUALLY Office 2003	0-7645-3980-9	$29.99
Teach Yourself VISUALLY Office XP	0-7645-0854-7	$29.99
Teach Yourself VISUALLY Mac OS X, Panther Edition	0-7645-4393-8	$29.99
Teach Yourself VISUALLY Photoshop 6	0-7645-3513-7	$29.99
Teach Yourself VISUALLY Photoshop 7	0-7645-3682-6	$29.99
Teach Yourself VISUALLY Photoshop Elements 2	0-7645-2515-8	$29.99
Teach Yourself VISUALLY PowerPoint 2002	0-7645-3660-5	$29.99
Teach Yourself VISUALLY Restoration and Retouching with Photoshop Elements 2	0-7645-2610-4	$29.99
Teach Yourself VISUALLY Windows 2000 Server	0-7645-3428-9	$29.99
Teach Yourself VISUALLY Windows Me Millennium Edition	0-7645-3495-5	$29.99
Teach Yourself VISUALLY Windows XP	0-7645-3619-2	$29.99
Teach Yourself VISUALLY Wireless Networking	0-7645-3413-X	$29.99
Teach Yourself VISUALLY Word 2002	0-7645-3587-0	$29.99
Teach Yourself Windows 95 VISUALLY	0-7645-6001-8	$29.99
Teach Yourself Windows 98 VISUALLY	0-7645-6025-5	$29.99
Teach Yourself Windows 2000 Professional VISUALLY	0-7645-6040-9	$29.99

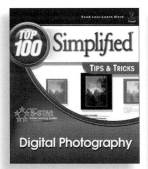
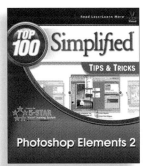

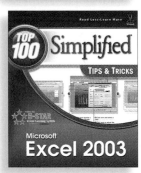

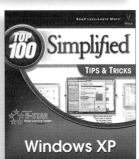
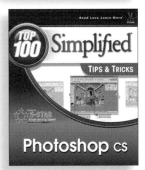 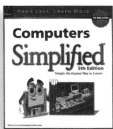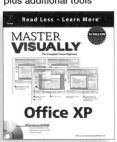

AE (autoexposure) Lock

A camera control that locks the exposure from a meter reading so the photographer can recompose the image and not change the exposure values.

AF (autofocus) Lock

A camera control that locks and holds the focus on a subject or object so the photographer can recompose the image.

ambient (available) light

Existing light in the scene.

angle of view

The amount or area "seen" by a lens or viewfinder measured in degrees. Shorter lenses have a greater field of view.

aperture

The size of the lens opening through which light passes. The size is adjusted by the diaphragm and size adjustments are expressed in f-stops.

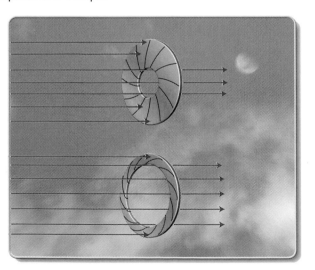

Aperture-Priority

A semi-automatic camera mode in which the photographer sets the aperture (f-stop) and the camera sets the shutter speed to achieve correct exposure.

artificial light

Light from an electric light or flash.

autofocus

A focus system that automatically focuses on the subject in either the selected auto focus area in the viewfinder or on the object in the center of the viewfinder.

back light

Light that comesrom behind the subject.

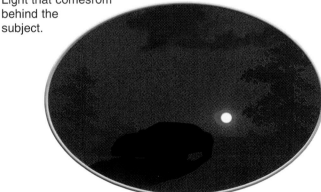

bit

The smallest unit of information usable by a computer. A single bit can represent one of two values; for example, black or white.

bit-depth

The number of bits used to represent each pixel in an image. Bit depth determines the pixel color and tonal range.

bounce light

Light that is directed toward an object such as a wall or ceiling and reflects onto the subject.

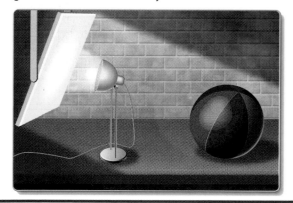

burn (burn in)

To make an area of an image darker by giving it more exposure.

charge-coupled device (CCD)

A light-sensitive device in digital cameras and scanners that captures the image.

cloning

The process of copying part of an image into another part of the image, used to remove or add objects to a digital image or to cover small imperfections.

CMYK

The four colors used by commercial printing presses: cyan, magenta, yellow, and black (K).

color balance

An image sensor's response to colors in a scene. Achieved in a digital camera by setting the white balance to match the primary light source in the scene.

color cast

The presence of an extraneous, usually unwanted, color tint in an image.

color temperature

The color of light measured in degrees Kelvin (K). Warm, light has a lower temperature. Cool light has a higher temperature.

compositing

The process of combining all or part of two or more digital images into a single image.

compression

A way to reduce file size. Lossy compression permanently discards information in the original file to reduce file size. Lossless compression does not discard information in the original file.

crop

To trim or discard one or more edges of an image.

depth of field

The zone or range of apparent sharpness in a photo. The range of sharpness generally extends one-third in front of and two-thirds behind the subject.

digital zoom

A method of making a subject appear closer by cropping away the edges of the scene.

dye sublimation

A photo printer that uses gaseous color dyes to create a continuous tone image that resembles a traditional photograph.

exposure compensation

A camera control that allows the photographer to overexpose (+ setting) or underexpose (- setting) images by a specified amount from the metered exposure.

fast

Refers to film or photo paper that is very sensitive to light. It also refers to a lens that offers a very wide aperture such as f/1.4 and a short shutter speed.

filter

A piece of glass or plastic placed over a camera lens to alter the light color or quality.

flat

Describes a scene, light, photograph, or negative that shows little difference between dark and light tones.

focal length

The distance from the optical center of the lens to the focal plane when the lens is focused on infinity. The longer the focal length is the greater the magnification.

focal point

The point on a focused image where rays of light intersect after reflecting from a single point on a subject.

focus

The point at which light rays from the lens converge to form a sharp image.

front light

Light that comes from behind or beside the camera to strike the front of the subject.

f-stop

A number that equals the focal length of the lens divided by the diameter of the aperture at a given setting.

grain

Undesirable multicolored flecks also referred to as "noise." Grain is most visible in high-speed film photos and in digital images captured at high ISO settings.

© 2004 Charlotte K. Lowrie

grayscale

A scale that shows black, white, and all intermediate tones of gray between. Also refers to rendering a digital image in black, white, and tones of gray.

hot shoe

A mount on a camera that accommodates a separate flash unit and allows communication between the camera and flash unit.

infinity

The farthest position on the distance scale of a lens (approximately 50 feet and beyond).

ISO rating

A rating that describes the sensitivity to light of film or an image sensor. ISO is expressed in numbers such as ISO 125.

JPEG

Joint Photographic Expert Group. A file format that compresses data by discarding information from the original file.

LCD

Liquid Crystal Display. Commonly used to describe the picture preview screen on digital cameras.

middle gray

An average gray that has 18 percent reflectance.

normal lens

A lens whose focus length is approximately the same as the diagonal measurement of the film or image sensor used.

optical zoom

Subject magnification that results from the lens.

Courtesy Nikon, Inc.

overexpose

To give more light to film or an image sensor than is required to adequately record the scene.

parallax

The difference between what the photographer sees through the viewfinder and what the lens sees.

pixel

Abbreviation for picture element. The smallest bit of information used in a digital image or produced by a device.

polarizing filter

A filter that reduces reflections from surfaces such as glass or water.

PPI

The number of pixels per linear inch or the resolution of a computer monitor, digital camera, or digital image.

RAM

Random Access Memory. The memory in a computer that temporarily stores information for rapid access.

reflected light meter

Measures light reflected from the subject.

reflector

A surface such as white cardboard used to redirect light into shadow areas of a scene or subject.

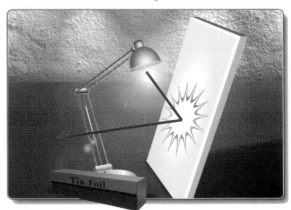

resampling
A method of averaging surrounding pixels to add or increase the number of pixels in a digital image.

resolution
The amount of information present in an image to represent detail in a digital image.

RGB
Red, Green, and Blue. A color model used to define the relative amounts of red, green, and blue components they contain.

sharp
The point in an image at which fine detail and textures are clear and well defined.

Shutter-Priority
A semi-automatic camera mode in which the photographer sets the shutter speed and the camera sets the aperture (f- stop) to achieve the correct exposure.

shutter
A mechanical device in the camera that regulates how long light is let into the camera to make an exposure. Measurements are expressed in seconds and fractions of seconds.

side light
Light that strikes the subject from the side.

slow
Refers to film and paper that requires relatively more light for exposure. Also refers to a lens that does not have a very wide aperture but has a long shutter speed.

SLR
Single Lens Reflex, a type of camera that enables the photographer to see the scene through the lens that takes the picture.

speed
Refers to a material's relative sensitivity to light. Also refers to the ability of a lens to let in more light by opening the lens to a wider aperture.

spot meter
Measures reflected light or brightness from a small portion of the subject.

telephoto effect
The effect telephoto lenses create that make objects appear to be closer together than they really are.

telephoto

A lens with a focal length longer than 50 to 60mm in 35mm format.

Courtesy Olympus USA

TIFF

Tagged Image File Format. A commonly used image format that supports 16.8 million colors and offers lossless compression to preserve all of the original file information.

top light

Light that strikes the subject from above, such as sunlight at midday.

© 2004 Charlotte K. Lowrie

TTL

Through The Lens, a system that reads the light passing through the lens that will expose the film or strike the image sensor.

tungsten lighting

Common household lighting that uses tungsten filaments. Without filtering or the correct white balance settings, pictures taken under tungsten light display a yellow-orange color cast.

underexpose

To provide less light to film or an image sensor than is required to adequately record the scene.

Unsharp Mask

In digital image editing, a filter that increases the apparent sharpness of the image. This filter cannot correct poor focus in the camera.

USB

Universal Serial Bus. A method for connecting peripheral devices to a computer at data transfer rates up to 12 Mbps (megabits per second).

viewfinder

A viewing system that allows the photographer to see all or part of the scene that will be included in the final picture.

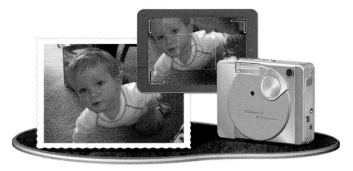

white balance

The relative intensity of red, green, and blue in a light source. White balance compensates for lights that are different from daylight to create correct color balance.

wide-angle distortion

The effect of making objects appear stretched or farther apart than they really are when a wide-angle lens is used at a close subject range.

© 2004 Charlotte K. Lowrie

wide-angle

A lens with a focal length shorter than 50 to 60mm in 35mm format.

INDEX

Clone Stamp tool (Photoshop Elements), 144
close-ups, sharpness, 75
CMOS (Complementary Metal-Oxide Semiconductor),
  defined, 7
color
  add selectively, 180
  adjust (edit images), 140–141, 233
  avoid color inaccurate casts, 107
  balance, 141
  cast, calibrate computer monitor, 116–119
  correct a cast (edit images), 142
  electronic flash, effect on, 29
  flood fill (edit image), 198–199
  grayscale, relationship to, 31
  light and, 28
  match screen and print, 232–233
  measurement, 30
  midday characteristics, 28
  sunrise characteristics, 28
  sunset characteristics, 29
  test picture evaluation, 95
  tint photos (edit images), 190
  white balance, 31
compact digital cameras, features, 16
compatibility, file formats, Photoshop Elements, 127
compensation, flash units, 34
Complementary Metal-Oxide Semiconductor (CMOS),
  defined, 7
composite photos, Photoshop Elements (Adobe) and,
  170–173
composition
  characteristics, 60–61
  control techniques, 66–67
  creative use of, 78–79
  design considerations, 62–63
  digital workflow, verification, 11
  focus lock and, 54
  traditional techniques, 64–65
  viewfinder compared to LCD, 55
compression
  lossless compared to lossy, 8
  telephoto lenses and, 46

computer
  image storage locations, 129
  images, download to, 92–93
  monitors, features, 23
  requirements for photo processing, 22
  transfer pictures to, 11
connections, printers, 25
contact sheet, print, 238–239
contrast, adjust (edit images), 138–139
cost
  advantages of digital photography, 4
  printers, 25
crooked photos, straightening, 152–153
crop photos
  Photoshop Elements (Adobe), 204–205
    add text, 208
    to print, 206
    straighten and, 207
    without Crop tool, 209
  reasons to, 202

D

darkroom (digital)
  printers, features, 24–25
  requirements, 22–23
date and time, camera setup, 87
delete, text, 163
depth of field
  composition techniques, 66
  enhance picture effects with, 70–73
  set, 40
design, composition, 62–63
desktop background, display photos as, 246–247
detail, maximize, 74
digital noise
  avoid, 109
  defined, 7
digital photography
  cost advantages, 4
  use suggestions, 4
  usefulness of, 4

INDEX

digital workflow
    clear memory, 13
    composition and exposure verification, 11
    computer, transfer pictures to, 11
    defined, 10
    edit pictures, 12
    image capture step, 10
    LCD, usefulness of, 11
    print and share pictures, 12
    store and organize pictures, 13
digital zoom
    compared to optical zoom, 48
    image quality and, 108
displays. See monitors (computer)
distortion, wide-angle lenses, 45
dodge and burn photos, Photoshop Elements (Adobe), 145
download images, images to computer, 92–93
DPI (dots per inch), defined, 224
drop shadows, add, 166
dust, remove (edit images), 143
DVD PictureShow (Ulead), slideshows, 5
DVDs (recordable)
    archiving and, 22
    slideshows, 5
    types, 23
dye-sublimation printers, features, 24

E

edit
    pictures, 12
    text, 162
Elliptical Marquee tool (Photoshop Elements), 185
e-mail
    photos, 250–251
    post, 5
enlargements, selecting photos for, 229
evaluation
    composition and, 60
    test pictures, 94–95
Excel (Microsoft), photo catalog, 268–269
exposure
    composition and, 78
    composition considerations, 61
    digital workflow, verification, 11

flash compensation, 34
    histograms and, 102–103
    light meters, characteristics, 30
    Photoshop Elements and, 169
exposure modes
    camera seclection and, 17
    types, 42–43

F

file formats
    camera setup, 87
    convert, 218–219
    e-mail photos, 250–251
    lossless compared to lossy, 8
    Photoshop Elements (Adobe), compatibility, 127
file size
    composite photos and, 171
    resize multiple, 220–221
fill flash
    create effects, 80
    flash units, 35
film grain, add, 156
filters, types, 21
fisheye lens effect, Photoshop Elements (Adobe), 179
fixed focus systems, features, 52
flash units
    color, effect on, 29
    compensation, 34
    create effects, 80
    distance considerations, 34
    features, 19
    fill flash, 35
    outdoor photography, 35
    troubleshoot, 91
    warm effect of, 83
flood fill, Photoshop Elements (Adobe), 198–199
fluorescent light, characteristics, 29
focal length
    depth of field, 40, 72
    features, 44
focus
    composition techniques, 66
    creative use of, 77
    depth of field, 40

INDEX

tripods
    avoid camera shake, 106
    features, 20
troubleshoot camera operation, 90–91
tungsten (household) light, characteristics, 29

U

Ulead DVD PictureShow, slideshows, 5
undo changes, Photoshop Elements (Adobe), 133
UV filters, usefulness of, 21

V

vertical text, add, 160–161
viewfinders
    compared to LCD, 55
    parallax, 49
vignettes, create (edit images), 184–186

W

Web sites
    photo gallery, create, 252–254
    photos, post, 5
    photo-sharing, upload to, 255–257
white balance
    camera setup, 87
    color casts, avois inaccurate, 107
    defined, 31
    set, 31

white point
    computer monitors, 119
    set (edit images), 136–137
wide-angle distortion, correct, 164
wide-angle lens
    depth of field, 40
    features, 45
wide-angle zoom lenses, depth of field, control, 71
Word (Microsoft), calendars, add photos, 266–267
workflow
    clear memory, 13
    composition and exposure verification, 11
    computer, transfer picture to, 11
    edit pictures, 12
    image capture step, 10
    introduction, 9
    LCD, usefulness of, 11
    print and share pictures, 12
    store and organize pictures, 13
workspace, Photoshop Elements (Adobe), 121

Z

zoom
    depth of field, 40
    optical compared to digital, 48
zoom lenses
    features, 47
    wide-angle, control depth of field, 71